From a Fig Leaf to a Righteous Robe

Joseph R. DiCostanzo

PUBLISHED *by* PARABLES
Earthly Stories with a Heavenly Meaning

Journey of Faith
Joseph R. DiCostanzo

Published By Parables
October, 2020

ISBN 978-1-951497-94-1
Printed in the United States of America

From a Fig Leaf to a Righteous Robe

Joseph R. DiCostanzo

PUBLISHED *by* PARABLES

Earthly Stories with a Heavenly Meaning

Contents

Joseph R. DiCostanzo

PREFACE

Journey of Faith is a compilation of selected entries taken from my personal journals written over several years. My intent was to prepare the book only to share with our children. After reading some of the entries in my journals, I was encouraged by my wife, Betty, and friends to consider publishing the writings for others who might be inspired and encouraged.

My Journey of Faith began when I learned that a Christian was not someone who went to church, but a person who accepted Jesus Christ as Lord and Savior of their life and maintained a personal relationship with Him. You will learn how I went from fearing God to respecting Him and learning of His unconditional love. You will discover what it means when I say I went from wearing a fig leaf to wearing a righteous robe.

I am grateful to the Holy Spirit for the inspirations I received during my quiet times with Him. The quiet times continue to be the best part of my day.

You will read personal prayers the Lord inspired me to write for our children and for my wife. The book includes psalms and songs that have yet to be set to music, and writings that were inspired by God's Word. There are poems, meditations, and reflections that were all influenced by God's Word and His creation.

Many of the writings include Bible references that are relevant to the text. I encourage the reader to check out the Scriptures and give the Lord the opportunity to minister to you through His Word.

Since the book was initially written for our children, I was not sure whether I should include information about my Mom and Dad. As you will discover, I decided to include the brief reflections as a tribute to them.

Life truly is a Journey of Faith. There is so little that we actually have control over. That is why we must pray for God's wisdom, and seek His will. We can trust our Lord. He tells us in Jeremiah 29:11- For I know the plans I have for you," declares the Lord, "plans to prosper you and not to harm you, plans to give you hope and a future.

I am convinced that, when we say we can't afford to take the time to spend with the Lord, the truth is we can't afford **not** to spend time with Him. You will find the day is much brighter and the burdens much lighter.

I thank my Lord and Savior, Jesus Christ, for accompanying me on my journey, and am certain He will be with me and for me as I continue my Journey of Faith.

I would like to thank our friend, Jackie Deda, who completed several pieces of original artwork that have been included in this book. The pictures she painted were inspirations she received while reading the draft document.

I dedicate this book to my awesome wife, Betty. She has been a faithful partner who generously dedicated many hours to assist with typing, editing and proofreading. Without her assistance and encouragement, this book would not yet be completed.

I pray that this book will inspire, challenge, and be an encouragement to you. I pray you are inspired to be intentional about making time to be in the presence of the Lord, and reading His Word every day. He will honor your commitment, and doing so will definitely have a positive impact on your life.

Joe DiCostanzo

Myrtle Beach, South Carolina

September 2020

Joseph R. DiCostanzo

Section 1

.

Poems

Joseph R. DiCostanzo

SERVING MY KING

EACH DAY IS A GIFT OF MY KING OF KINGS
A NEW VERSE IN MY SONG I LOVE TO SING
I KNOW ALL I HAVE, AND MAY CALL MY OWN
IT'S NOT REALLY MINE, BUT IS HIS ALONE   Deut 10:14

I'VE LEARNED WHAT IT MEANS TO BE TRULY FREE
IT'S SERVING MY KING EACH DAY FAITHFULLY
FORSAKING ALL ELSE TO ANSWER HIS CALL
HOLDING NOTHING BACK, GIVING HIM MY ALL   Luke 10:27

I TRY TO REMEMBER EACH DAY THAT I LIVE
IT'S GOOD TO RECEIVE, BUT BETTER TO GIVE
BY GIVING TO OTHERS WHO ARE IN NEED
OUT OF HIS ABUNDANCE HE GIVES TO ME   Luke 6:38

EACH TIME I CONFESS MY SINS TO MY LORD
HE FORGIVES ME, AND OUR FRIENDSHIP RESTORED
I'M HUMBLED BY HIS COMPASSION AND LOVE
HIS MERCY AND GRACE TRUE GIFTS FROM ABOVE   Rom 10:9-10

MY REFRAIN:
I'LL PRAISE YOU, MY KING, EACH DAY THAT I LIVE
EACH DAY I HAVE BREATH I'LL HAVE SOMETHING TO GIVE
CONTINUE TO LEAD ME SO I WILL KNOW
I'M ON THE PATH WHERE YOU WANT ME TO GO   Pro 3:5-6

Joseph R. DiCostanzo

WAITING ON THE LORD

WHILE I'M HERE WAITING, AND ABLE TO SEE
MAY I ALWAYS ADMIRE EACH FLOWER AND TREE

WHILE I'M HERE WAITING, AND ABLE TO SPEAK
MAY I SHARE CHRIST'S LOVE WITH ALL WHOM I MEET

WHILE I'M HERE WAITING, AND ABLE TO PRAY
MAY I INTERCEDE FOR OTHERS EACH DAY

WHILE I'M HERE WAITING, AND ABLE TO HEAR
MAY I FOLLOW CHRIST'S LEADING WITHOUT ANY FEAR

WHILE I'M HERE WAITING, AND ABLE TO STAND
MAY I ALWAYS BE WILLING TO GIVE OTHERS A HAND

WHILE I'M HERE WAITING, AND ABLE TO SHARE
MAY WHAT I DO FOR OTHERS SHOW THEM I CARE

WHILE I'M HERE WAITING, AND YOU GIVE ME BREATH
I'LL PRAISE AND HONOR YOU 'TIL I TAKE MY LAST BREATH

A MIGHTY ENCOUNTER WITH CHRIST
MERY CHRISTMAS

DID YOU EVER CONTEMPLATE
THAT CHRISTMAS IS A SPECIAL DATE
WHEN CHRISTIANS CHOOSE TO CELEBRATE
THE DAY THAT CHRIST WAS BORN

IF NOT FOR CHRIST, THERE IS NO REASON
TO EVEN HAVE A CHRISTMAS SEASON
AND I WOULD NOT BE A REDEEMED MAN
HAD CHRIST NOT DIED FOR ME

YET NOW I SEE A MULTITUDE
WHO SEEM TO HAVE THE ATTITUDE
THAT SOMEHOW I AM BEING RUDE
WHEN I SAY "MERRY CHRISTMAS"

I JUST WANT TO REMIND YOU ALL
THIS SEASON WOULD NOT EXIST AT ALL
IF CHRIST WAS NOT PREPARED TO GIVE HIS ALL
WHEN HE WAS BORN ON CHRISTMAS

SO DON'T TELL ME I CANNOT SAY
"MERRY CHRISTMAS" TO OBSERVE THE DAY
CHRIST PAID A DEBT I COULD NOT PAY
I LIVE MY LIFE FOR JESUS

THE GIFTS, LIGHTS, AND HOLIDAY CHEER
NON-CHRISTIANS LOOK FORWARD TO EACH YEAR
ARE NOT WHAT CHRISTIANS FIND SO DEAR
AS CELEBRATING THE BIRTH OF CHRIST

PERHAPS ONLY CHRISTIANS SHOULD OBSERVE CHRISTMAS DAY
AND NON-CHRISTIANS GO ABOUT THEIR WAY
PERMIT ME TO HONOR CHRIST MY WAY
ON THIS BLESSED DAY CALLED CHRISTMAS

MY PRAYER IS THAT YOU WOULD BELIEVE
CONFESS JESUS AS LORD AND SAVIOR AND RECEIVE
HIM INTO YOUR HEART AND NOT BE DECEIVED
THEN YOU AND I CAN BOTH SAY "MERRY CHRISTMAS"

PEER PRESSURE

DOING AS OTHERS SAY
JUST TO BE ACCEPTED
IS NOT THE RIGHT MOTIVE
YOU'LL SOON BE REJECTED

NOT SHARING YOUR THOUGHTS
WHEN YOU DON'T AGREE
IS COMPROMISING
A TRUTH YOU BELIEVE

WHEN YOU ARE TEMPTED
TO DO WHAT IS WRONG
BECAUSE OF PEER PRESSURE
YOU MUST REMAIN STRONG

WHEN YOU ONLY DO
WHAT OTHERS EXPECT
THEIR GAIN IS YOUR LOSS
YOUR LOSS IS RESPECT

WHEN ALL'S SAID AND DONE
YOU KNOW YOU'VE DONE RIGHT
WHEN THE ONE WHO IS PLEASED
IS THE LORD, JESUS CHRIST

"Have I not commanded you? Be strong and courageous. Do not be afraid; do not be discouraged, for the LORD your God will be with you wherever you go." Joshua 1:9

A NEW HEART – A FRESH START

SOME SAY "MAN" IS BASICALLY GOOD
AND THINGS SOMETIMES GO AWRY
WE KNOW THAT "**TRUTH**" IS WHAT'S GOOD
SO WHO TAUGHT MAN TO LIE

WHEN SOMEONE DOES WRONG
DOES NOT ACT AS HE SHOULD
COULD IT ALL BE HIS FAULT
IF HE IS BASICALLY GOOD?

GOD'S FINEST CREATION
DIDN'T OBEY AS HE SHOULD
BECAUSE OF HIS FAILURE
MAN WAS NO LONGER "GOOD"

AND ALL MAN HAS TRIED
HAS FAILED TO SUCCEED
TO CHANGE MAN'S BEHAVIOR
UNLESS HE TRULY BELIEVES

WHEN GOD SAW THAT MAN
WOULD NEED A NEW START
HE HAD A PLAN
THAT WOULD CHANGE A MAN'S HEART

HE SENT HIS SON JESUS
TO MAKE RIGHT WHAT WAS WRONG
HE'LL FORGIVE OUR TRANSGRESSIONS
AND GIVE US A NEW SONG

WE MUST BE WILLING
TO SERVE HIM EACH DAY
FOR UNTO GOD'S FAITHFUL
LIFE IS CHANGED – NOT TAKEN AWAY

"I will give you a new heart and put a new spirit in you; I will remove from you your heart of stone and give you a heart of flesh. And I will put my Spirit in you and move you to follow my decrees and be careful to keep my laws."
Ezk. 36:26-27

MAYBE

MAYBE YOU FEEL IT'S ALL UP TO YOU
THAT YOU ARE IN CONTROL OF YOUR LIFE
AND NO ONE HAS THE RIGHT TO SAY
WHAT YOU ARE DOING IS WRONG OR RIGHT

YOU MAY THINK YOU'RE THE LORD OF YOUR LIFE
BUT YOU ARE NOT THE LORD OF LORDS
AND NO MATTER WHAT YOU MAY THINK
YOU WILL NOT HAVE THE FINAL WORD

MAYBE YOU DON'T NEED ADVICE FROM OTHERS
YOU CAN FIGURE THINGS OUT FOR YOURSELF
IF YOU WORK LONG AND HARD ENOUGH
YOU WILL ACCUMULATE MUCH WEALTH

THERE IS A GOD WHO KNOWS ALL THINGS
SEEK THE COUNSEL HE HAS TO OFFER
HIS YOKE IS EASY AND HIS BURDEN LIGHT
HIS DESIRE IS TO SEE YOU PROSPER

MAYBE YOU FEEL OTHERS ARE USING YOU
TO FULFILL THEIR SELFISH DESIRES
AND WHEN THEY NO LONGER NEED YOUR HELP
THEY'LL LEAVE YOU IN THE MUCK AND MIRE

IT'S TRUE GOD HAS A PLAN FOR YOUR LIFE
HE WILL STAY WITH YOU 'TIL THE END
AND IF YOU CHOOSE TO FOLLOW HIS PLAN
HE WILL REWARD YOU AND CALL YOU HIS FRIEND

MAYBE YOU FEEL LIKE GIVING UP
YOU HAVE TRIED ALL YOU KNOW TO DO
THERE'S NOTHING LEFT WORTH LIVING FOR
LIFE HAS NO MEANING FOR YOU

WITH JESUS AS THE LORD OF YOUR LIFE
LIFE TAKES ON A WHOLE NEW MEANING
STRENGTH AND WISDOM WILL COME FROM ABOVE
'CAUSE YOU'RE A PRECIOUS CHILD OF THE KING

GOD WANTS YOUR ATTENTION

GOD WANTS YOUR ATTENTION
WITHOUT HESITATION OR RATIONALIZATION

TO GIVE NEW DIRECTION
AND TO EXPERIENCE HIS AFFECTION

IN HIM THERE IS NO DECEPTION
OR EXPLOITATION

JUST ILLUMINATION AND CONSOLATION
FOR OPTIMIZATION AND GRATIFICATION

YOUR EDUCATION OR REPUTATION
IS NOT A QUALIFICATION FOR GOD'S INTERVENTION

YOUR PERCEPTION MAY LEAD TO DECEPTION
OR EVEN EXAGGERATION

LEADING TO RAMIFICATIONS
THAT CAUSE SEPARATION

ACCEPT THE LORD'S INVITATION
WITHOUT PROCRASTINATION

HE MAY BRING CONVICTION
BUT NOT CONDEMNATION

UPON YOUR IDENTIFICATION
AS A CITIZEN IN GOD'S NATION

YOU WILL EXPERIENCE SATISFACTION,
PROPITIATION AND JUSTIFICATION

SO MAKE THE DECLARATION
KNOWING HIS DEATH AND RESURRECTION

HAS MADE JESUS CHRIST YOUR ONLY SALVATION!

Joseph R. DiCostanzo

WE STILL DO
(LOVE EACH OTHER)

A MORNING HUG, A TENDER KISS
HOW WOULD I FACE THE DAY WITHOUT HER
LOVED HER THEN, NOW, AND ALWAYS WILL
NO MATTER WHAT, I'LL LOVE HER STILL

WHEN SHE PUTS HER ARM IN MINE
I FEEL LIKE I'M TEN FEET TALL
I LOVE TO SEE THAT BEAUTIFUL SMILE ON HER FACE
AND TRULY ENJOY AN EXTENDED EMBRACE

OUR CHILDREN HAVE ENHANCED OUR LIVES
WITH FUN TIMES, CHALLENGES AND OPPORTUNITIES
WE DID OUR BEST TO SHARE GOD'S LOVE IN EACH LIFE
PRAYED GOD'S WISDOM AGAINST DECEPTION AND STRIFE

THERE HAVE BEEN SOME DIFFICULT TIMES
AND WE HAVE SHED MANY TEARS TOGETHER
BUT GOD'S PRESENCE HAS SEEN US THROUGH
HIS PROMISES ARE TRIED AND TRUE

SHE SENSES THINGS I NEVER COULD
AND DOES NOT WAIVER FROM THE TRUTH
SHE IS A SIGNIFICANT PART OF MY LIFE
I'VE COME TO HONOR, RESPECT AND CHERISH MY WIFE

KNOWLEDGE OF GOD

MAN SAYS, "KNOWLEDGE IS POWER"
AND HE SPEAKS RIGHTLY SO
BUT OUR GOD IS THE GOD ALL-KNOWING
HE PORTIONS OUT WHAT WE KNOW

THE EARTH IS FILLED WITH KNOWLEDGE
YES, KNOWLEDGE OF GOD'S GLORY
HE MADE EVERYTHING UNDER THE SUN
THAT'S THE TRUTH, NOT JUST A STORY

WE MAY IN OUR ARROGANCE
TAKE THE CREDIT ALONG LIFE'S COURSE
BUT ULTIMATELY ALL WILL ADMIT
THE GOD OF KNOWLEDGE IS OUR SOURCE

MAN WILL ONE DAY UNDERSTAND
ALL KNOWLEDGE THAT HE GAINS
HAS ALWAYS BEEN THERE TO BE LEARNED
THE TRUTH BE KNOWN - OUR GOD REIGNS!

BE SURE!

I OFTEN MUST REMIND MYSELF
THINGS ARE NOT ALWAYS AS THEY APPEAR
AND SOMETIMES WHEN OTHERS ARE SPEAKING
WHAT THEY ARE SAYING IS NOT WHAT I HEAR

INSTEAD OF GETTING A CONFIRMATION
WHEN I THINK THAT I UNDERSTAND
I'VE MADE THE MISTAKE OF DOING MY THING
AND RECEIVING A REPRIMAND

IT'S BEST NOT TO MAKE AN ASSUMPTION
THOUGH I'VE DONE THE SAME THING IN THE PAST
THINGS CAN CHANGE FROM DAY TO DAY
SO WHEN I'M NOT SURE - I ASK

WHEN I KNOW ALL THE DETAILS
I AVOID DISSENSION AND STRIFE
AND LIVE IN PEACE AND HARMONY
WITH ALL WHO COME INTO MY LIFE

YES ... REALLY

YES - GOD REALLY DID
SEND JESUS HIS SON
TO DIE FOR US ALL
EACH AND EVERYONE

YES - GOD REALLY LOVES
WITH NO STRINGS ATTACHED
AND ALWAYS WILL
HIS LOVE HAS NO MATCH

YES - GOD REALLY CARES
HE MEETS EVERY NEED
JUST ACKNOWLEDGE HIM
THERE'S NO NEED TO PLEAD

YES - GOD REALLY SAID
HE WILL FORGIVE
IF WE REPENT
AND FOR HIM LIVE

YES - GOD REALLY KNOWS
ABOUT YOU AND ME
HE LOVES US STILL
UNCONDITIONALLY

YES – GOD'S REALLY ALL-POWERFUL
YET GENTLE AND MEEK
KIND AND FORGIVING
TRUE FRIEND OF THE WEAK

YES - GOD REALLY SEES
MORE THAN YOU KNOW
NOTHING IS HIDDEN
WE REAP WHAT WE SOW

YES - GOD REALLY MEANS
THAT WE MUST OBEY
ALL HIS COMMANDS
NOT DO AS WE MAY

YES - GOD REALLY BLESSES
BEYOND ALL MEASURE
SHARING HIS KINGDOM
IS OUR GOD'S PLEASURE

YES - GOD REALLY IS
BELIEVE IT, OR NOT
ONE DAY YOU WILL SEE HIM
GIVE IT SOME THOUGHT

IT'S NOT ABOUT ME

I DON'T WANT TO BE LIKE AN EMPTY VINE
LIVING ONLY FOR MYSELF.
CONSUMING ALL THE LORD HAS PROVIDED
OR STORING IT ON A SHELF   HOSEA 10:1

NOT HOARDING MORE THAN WHAT I NEED
WHILE OTHERS DO WITHOUT.
GIVE AND IT SHALL BE GIVEN TO YOU
THAT'S WHAT IT'S ALL ABOUT   LUKE 6:38

I REALLY DON'T WANT TO SPEND MY TIME
ON THINGS THAT DO NOT LAST
BUT INVEST MY TIME IN THE LIVES OF OTHERS
'TIL MY LIFE ON EARTH HAS PASSED   JOHN 5:24

IT'S EASY TO GET CAUGHT UP IN MYSELF
THINKING I'M NUMBER ONE
BUT READING HIS WORD MAKES IT VERY CLEAR
I OWE IT ALL TO GOD'S SON   MATTHEW 6:33,
                                        MATHEW 19:30

MY REFRAIN
I THANK YOU, LORD, FOR ALL LIFE'S BLESSINGS
I AM BLESSED ABUNDANTLY
MAY I FREELY GIVE WITH A CHEERFUL HEART
AS YOU HAVE GIVEN TO ME   MATTHEW 10:8

NO MATTER

NO MATTER WHAT – RAIN OR SHINE
IN TIMES OF NEED OR WHEN ALL IS FINE

WHETHER IN SICKNESS OR IN HEALTH
IN TIMES OF POVERTY OR WEALTH

I'LL LOVE YOU LORD UNTIL THE END
YOU'VE BEEN A FAITHFUL AND TRUE FRIEND

Joseph R. DiCostanzo

HOW CAN IT BE...AND NOT BELIEVE

HOW CAN IT BE THAT ONE CAN SEE
   THE MOON AND STARLIT SKY
AND NOT BELIEVE THAT THERE'S A GOD
   WHO IS ON HIS THRONE ON HIGH

HOW CAN IT BE THAT ONE COULD PICK
   FROM A BUSH A BEAUTIFUL FLOWER
AND NOT BELIEVE THAT THERE'S A GOD
   WHO HAS CREATIVE POWER

HOW CAN IT BE THAT ONE COULD WATCH
   A MOTHER GIVE BIRTH TO HER CHILD
AND NOT BELIEVE THAT THERE'S A GOD
   WHO IS AWESOME YET MEEK AND MILD

HOW CAN IT BE THAT ONE COULD STAND
   UPON THE OCEAN SHORE
AND NOT BELIEVE THAT THERE'S A GOD
   WHO CONTROLS THE TIDES AND SO MUCH MORE

HOW CAN IT BE THAT ONE COULD HEAR
   OTHERS SPEAK OF THEIR SALVATION
AND NOT BELIEVE THAT THERE'S A GOD
   CAPABLE OF RE-CREATION

HOW CAN IT BE THAT ONE COULD PLANT
   A SEED AND GROW A TREE
AND NOT BELIEVE THAT THERE'S A GOD
   WHO CAN MEET OUR EVERY NEED

HOW CAN IT BE THAT WE COULD FEEL
   THE WARMTH OF THE SUN ON OUR FACE
AND NOT BELIEVE THAT THERE'S A GOD
   WHO PUT THE HEAVENLIES IN THEIR PLACE

HOW CAN IT BE THAT ONE COULD FEEL
   THE PULSE OF THEIR BEATING HEART
AND NOT BELIEVE THAT THERE'S A GOD
   WHO CAUSED THE BEATING TO START

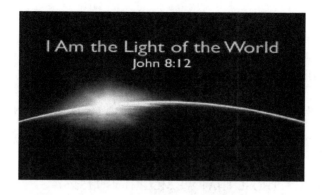

THE LIGHT (JESUS) -VS-THE SHADOW

WHEN YOU SEE YOUR SHADOW
IN YOUR LINE OF SIGHT
YOU ARE LOOKING TOWARDS THE DARKNESS
AND NOT TOWARDS **THE** LIGHT

SHADOWS WILL FOLLOW
WHEREVER WE GO
BUT THEY DON'T NEED TO HAUNT US
AS LONG AS WE KNOW...

THAT THOUGH OUR SHADOW
SEEMS A FEARFUL SIGHT
THEY ALL ARE RENDERED HARMLESS
WHEN EXPOSED TO **THE** LIGHT

THE LIGHT REVEALS THE SHADOWS
EACH AND EVERY ONE
BUT **THE** LIGHT OVERCOMES THE DARKNESS
THANKS TO GOD'S ONLY SON

EVEN WALKING THROUGH THE VALLEY
OF THE SHADOW OF DEATH
THE LIGHT WILL CONTINUE TO LEAD YOU
BEYOND YOUR LAST BREATH

TAKE YOUR EYES OFF THE SHADOW
AND TURNED TOWARDS **THE** LIGHT
HE GETS BRIGHTER AND BRIGHTER
WHEN YOU KEEP HIM IN SIGHT

21

HOLY SPIRIT

THE HOLY SPIRIT IS OUR ADVOCATE
WHO WILL STAY WITH US FOREVER (JOHN 14:16)
HE WILL TEACH US ALL WE NEED TO KNOW
AND HELP US TO REMEMBER (JOHN 14:26)

HE'S THE SPIRIT OF TRUTH, THE FAITHFUL ONE (JOHN 15:26)
HE IS OUR SOURCE OF PEACE (JOHN 14:27)
WE ARE TO TESTIFY OF HIM
TO ALL THOSE THAT WE MEET (JOHN 15:26)

HE CONVICTS US OF SIN
THAT WE MIGHT BECOME RIGHTEOUS IN HIS SIGHT (JN 16:8)
HE ALONE IS THE FINAL JUDGE (JOHN 16:9)
WHO DETERMINES WHAT'S WRONG AND RIGHT

HE GUIDES US IN THE TRUTH,
BECAUSE HIS WORDS COME FROM THE FATHER (JN 16:13)
HE KNOWS WHAT IS YET TO COME (JOHN 16:13)
KNOWING WHAT'S BEST FOR HIS SONS AND DAUGHTERS

FROM THE LAW OF SIN AND DEATH
HE DOES SET US FREE (ROMANS 8:2)
AND WHEN WE DON'T KNOW WHAT TO PRAY
FOR US HE INTERCEDES (ROMANS 8:26, 27)

**THANK YOU, FATHER
...PRAISE YOU, JESUS
...COME HOLY SPIRIT**

MY AWESOME WIFE

THE WORD SAYS TO LOVE YOUR WIFE
        AS CHRIST HAS LOVED THE CHURCH,
KNOWING HE GAVE HIS LIFE FOR US,
        PROVES HE KNOWS HOW MUCH YOU ARE WORTH.

YOU ARE A TRUE AND FAITHFUL FRIEND,
        AND A MOST AWESOME WIFE,
I PROMISE TO LOVE, CHERISH AND BE THERE FOR YOU
        FOR THE REST OF MY EARTHLY LIFE.

OUR CHILDREN ARE ESPECIALLY BLESSED
        WITH THE VERY BEST "MUM" EVER,
YOU HAVE LOVED AND SACRIFICED FOR THEM
        WITH NO RESERVATIONS WHATSOEVER.

I THANK THE LORD FOR YOU, MY LOVE,
        AND FOR ALL THAT WE HAVE SHARED,
MY LIFE HAS BEEN MADE COMPLETE WITH YOU
        A BEAUTIFUL MATE WHO HAS ALWAYS CARED.

LORD, BLESS MY WIFE AS SO MANY THROUGH HER
        HAVE OFTENTIMES BEEN BLESSED,
ALTHOUGH I AM SO UNDESERVING
        YOU HAVE BLESSED ME WITH THE BEST!

Joseph R. DiCostanzo

Section 2

Prayers

Joseph R. DiCostanzo

LORD, I HAVE THIS SITUATION...(1)

LORD, I HAVE THIS SITUATION
PLEASE HELP ME TO UNDERSTAND
AFTER BEING BLESSED WITH A BEAUTIFUL CHILD
I SEE HIM STRUGGLING AS A MAN

HIS HEART WAS TENDER, HIS MANNER MILD
HE WAS THOUGHTFUL, LOVING, AND KIND
INNOVATIVE EVEN WHEN PLAYING WITH TOYS
HE WAS BLESSED WITH A CREATIVE MIND

BUT SOME THINGS HAPPENED IN HIS LIFE
THAT CHANGED THE CHILD I KNEW
HE MADE DECISIONS THAT WERE NOT WISE
ULTIMATELY REJECTING YOU

I KNOW THAT I DID SOME THINGS WRONG
BUT I DID WHAT I THOUGHT WAS BEST
IF I COULD, I WOULD CHANGE SOME THINGS
I FEEL LIKE I JUST FAILED A TEST

NOW HE STRUGGLES AND SEEMS SO LOST
ARE THERE WORDS THAT CAN BE SPOKEN?
TO HELP HIM THROUGH THESE DIFFICULT TIMES
AND HEAL ALL THOSE THINGS THAT SEEM BROKEN?

LORD, I HAVE RUN OUT OF WORDS TO SAY
AND THERE IS NOTHING I KNOW TO DO
SO I TURN TO YOU, MY SOVEREIGN GOD
'CAUSE NOTHING'S TOO DIFFICULT FOR YOU

INTO YOUR HANDS I COMMIT OUR SON
I PRAY HE WILL ACKNOWLEDGE YOU
HEAL HIS BODY AND RENEW HIS MIND
I KNOW ALL CAN BE RESTORED BY YOU

28

LORD, I HAVE THIS SITUATION...(2)

LORD, I HAVE THIS SITUATION
IT'S ABOUT A SPECIAL MAN
WHO HAS SOME THINGS TO OVERCOME
THINGS I DON'T FULLY UNDERSTAND

I'VE TRIED ALL I KNOW TO DO
I BELIEVE I'VE DONE MY BEST
SOMETHING MORE NEEDS TO BE DONE
WOULD YOU PLEASE DO THE REST?

YOUR POWER IS MUCH GREATER
THAN THAT OF ANYONE I KNOW
HE REALLY NEEDS A TOUCH FROM YOU
HE IS FEELING MIGHTY LOW

RESTORE HIS MIND THAT HE MIGHT KNOW
THE TRUTH THAT SETS HIM FREE
IMPART TO HIM YOUR WISDOM, LORD
OPEN HIS EYES YOUR PLANS TO SEE

HELP HIM SEE WHAT'S IN THE PAST
DOESN'T DETERMINE WHAT'S IN STORE
THOUGH ALL HE HAD MAY HAVE BEEN LOST
HIS FUTURE HOLDS SO MUCH MORE

GIVE HIM THE STRENGTH TO CARRY ON
AND THE PEACE ONLY YOU CAN GIVE
A VISION FOR HIS FUTURE
AND THE WILL TO FORGIVE AND LIVE

I TRUST THAT YOU KNOW WHAT IS BEST
I NEED YOUR GUIDANCE EVERY DAY
TO HELP HIM BEGIN HIS LIFE ANEW
I LOOK TO YOU TO SHOW THE WAY

Joseph R. DiCostanzo

A PARENT'S PRAYER FOR A SON

LORD, I SIT HERE IN YOUR PRESENCE
IT'S REALLY NOT ABOUT ME
IT CONCERNS OUR FIRST-BORN SON
HAVING THOUGHTS OF HOW THINGS COULD BE

YOU GIFTED HIM IN MANY WAYS
A HEALTHY BODY AND SOUND MIND
HE HAS A HEART FOR FAMILY AND FRIENDS
HIS MANNER IS FRIENDLY AND KIND

YOU'VE OPENED DOORS THAT HE MIGHT BE
THE FINE DOCTOR HE HAS BECOME
I PRAY HE SEEKS DIRECTION FROM YOU
THAT YOUR WILL AND HIS ARE ONE

HE MAY NOT ALWAYS THINK THINGS THROUGH
HE MAY SOMETIMES ACT IN HASTE
MAY HE LOOK TO YOU FOR WISDOM
THROUGH THE CHALLENGES HE WILL FACE

THIS IS AN UNSETTLING TIME IN HIS LIFE
AS HE DECIDES WHAT HE IS TO DO
I PRAY THAT HE PRAYS "YOUR WILL BE DONE"
AND HE DOES NOTHING WITHOUT SEEKING YOU

I PRAY HE WILL FIND TRUE CONTENTMENT
IN ALL THAT HE HAS ACHIEVED
ALWAYS MINDFUL OF YOUR FAITHFULNESS
AND THE MANY BLESSINGS HE HAS RECEIVED

YOU HAVE A PERFECT PLAN FOR HIS LIFE
AS HE SERVES YOU HE WILL PROSPER
FOR IN YOU ARE HIS FUTURE AND HOPE
MAY HE SEEK ALL YOU HAVE TO OFFER

A HUSBAND'S PRAYER

LORD, I SIT HERE IN YOUR PRESENCE
   THINKING OF MY AWESOME WIFE
WHO HAS BEEN MY HELP-MATE AND FAITHFUL FRIEND
   AND HAS TRULY BLESSED MY LIFE

BECAUSE SHE SEEKS YOUR WISDOM
   AND SENSES WHEN THINGS AREN'T RIGHT
SHE CAN SEE THINGS NOT AS THEY APPEAR
   LED BY YOUR SPIRIT – NOT BY HER SIGHT

SHE HAS ALWAYS MADE OUR HOUSE A HOME
   EVEN WHEN TIMES WERE LEAN
FAITHFULLY TENDING TO ALL NEEDING DONE
   MUCH OF WHICH GOES UNSEEN

OUR CHILDREN ARE VERY FORTUNATE
   TO HAVE HER AS THEIR MOTHER
SHE HAS ALWAYS BEEN THEIR BIGGEST FAN
   AND SUPPORTS THEM LIKE NO OTHER

SHE CONSIDERS THE NEEDS OF OTHERS
   AHEAD OF WHAT SHE DESIRES
FREELY GIVING WITH A JOYFUL HEART
   IN A MANNER THAT TRULY INSPIRES

MY DESIRE IS TO BLESS HER
   AS MUCH AS I AM ABLE
THAT SHE WILL ALWAYS SENSE MY LOVE FOR HER
   IS TRUE, SURE AND STABLE

I PRAY YOU WILL GRANT THE TWO OF US
   MANY MORE DAYS TO SHARE
THAT IN OUR LIVES YOU ARE GLORIFIED
   HONORED ALWAYS AND EVERYWHERE

I PRAY YOU WILL GRANT MY LOVE
   THE DESIRES OF HER HEART
REWARD HER FOR HER FAITHFULNESS
   THAT'S BEEN STEADFAST FROM THE START

INTENTIONAL

LORD,

IT IS MY INTENTION TO SERVE YOU
BY SERVING OTHERS IN NEED
PROMPT ME AS TO WHAT I SHOULD DO
I WILL FOLLOW – YOU TAKE THE LEAD

IT IS MY INTENTION TO LOVE YOU
AND SHOW YOUR LOVE FOR OTHERS THROUGH ME
OVERLOOKING WHAT OTHERS MAY DO OR SAY
AND LOVING THEM UNCONDITIONALLY

IT IS MY INTENTION TO HONOR YOU
GIVING YOU THE PRAISE THAT IS DUE
BECAUSE ALL I AM OR EVER HOPE TO BE
I OWE IT ALL TO YOU

IT IS MY INTENTION TO BE IN YOUR WILL
AND DO ALL YOU REQUIRE OF ME
TO DO JUSTLY AND LOVE MERCY
AND ALWAYS WALK HUMBLY WITH THEE

IT IS MY INTENTION TO TRUST YOU
YOU HAVE BEEN EVER-FAITHFUL AND TRUE
WHEN I DON'T KNOW WHICH WAY TO TURN
I KNOW I CAN COUNT ON YOU

IT IS MY INTENTION TO BE FAITHFUL
REPENTANT, FORGIVING AND TRUE
IT IS MY INTENTION TO SPEND ETERNITY
WITH FAMILY, FRIENDS AND YOU!

LESSONS LEARNED
2 COR 10:5

LORD, I KNOW THAT I HAVE FAILED YOU
   TIME AND TIME AGAIN
TAKING MY CHANCES, DOING MY THING
   KNOWING WITHOUT YOU I COULD NOT WIN

I'VE MADE DECISIONS WITHOUT YOU
   THEY WERE NOT THE BEST
THEY BROUGHT DISCOURAGEMENT AND TURMOIL
   BROKEN RELATIONSHIPS AND DISTRESS

I HAVE SAID THINGS THAT HURT OTHERS
   NOT CAPTURING MY THOUGHTS
HURTING THOSE I LOVE THE MOST
   NOT SPEAKING WORDS OF LIFE, AS I OUGHT

I'VE DONE THINGS I NOW REGRET
   AND NOT DONE THINGS I KNEW TO DO
TAKING CONTROL OF SITUATIONS
   INSTEAD OF SEEKING WISDOM FROM YOU

LORD, HELP ME, I PRAY, TO REMEMBER
   THAT BEFORE ANYTHING I SAY OR DO
I WILL CAPTURE MY THOUGHTS, SEEK YOUR WISDOM
   TO BRING ALL HONOR AND GLORY TO YOU

Lord
I pray
to be *Led* to
and by you

"…and we take captive every thought to make it obedient to Christ."
2 Cor 10:5

MY PRAYER
(INSPIRED BY GOD'S WORDS TO ZECHARIAH)

TOO OFTEN, LORD, YOU TAKE NO PLEASURE IN ME. BUT YOU
CONTINUE TO CALL ME TO YOURSELF. WAITING FOR ME TO
REPENT AND MAKE THE FIRST MOVE. READY TO GREET ME,
FORGIVE ME AND RESTORE MY RELATIONSHIP WITH YOU.

JUST AS YOU PROMISED TO BE A WALL OF FIRE AROUND
JERUSALEM AND TO BE ITS GLORY WITHIN, I PRAY YOU WILL BE A
WALL OF FIRE AROUND OUR HOME AND YOUR HOLY SPIRIT WILL
BE EVER PRESENT WITHIN.

MAY YOU FIND ME WORTHY - ONLY BECAUSE OF THE SACRIFICE
OF YOUR PRECIOUS SON, JESUS - TO BE CONSIDERED AN APPLE OF
YOUR EYE - YOUR INHERITANCE. I CONFESS MY WEAKNESS, AND
KNOW WHATEVER I ACCOMPLISH IS NOT BY MY MIGHT OR BY MY
POWER - BUT BY YOUR SPIRIT.

I HUMBLY ASK FOR A FRESH ANOINTING OF YOUR SPIRIT THAT I
MIGHT SERVE YOU WELL. USE ME TO HELP MAKE A DESOLATE
PLACE PLEASANT ONCE AGAIN. USE ME TO OFFER HOPE TO THE
HOPELESS. MAY I NEVER COMPROMISE BY COMMISSION OR
OMISSION, BUT HELP ME TO BE BOLD (NOT FEARFUL) AND STRONG
(NOT WEAK). MAY I ALWAYS SPEAK THE TRUTH IN LOVE AND TO
RENDER TRUE AND SOUND JUDGMENT. MAY I NEVER PLOT EVIL
OR SWEAR FALSELY - BUT LOVE PEACE AND TRUTH.

MAY OTHERS BE DRAWN TO YOU, LORD, WHEN THEY WITNESS
HOW YOU LOVE AND CARE FOR YOUR CHILDREN - INCLUDING
THIS CHILD. I DECLARE THE VICTORY, BECAUSE YOU, LORD
ALMIGHTY, ARE MY GOD!

I PRAY THESE THINGS IN THE NAME OF YOUR PRECIOUS SON,
JESUS CHRIST. AMEN.

SENSES

<u>MY REFRAIN:</u>
MAY YOUR SPIRIT WITHIN ME TAKE OVER MY SENSES
 SO IT'S NOT ALL ABOUT ME
WHOMEVER YOU PLACE IN MY PATH WILL SENSE,
 WHAT IT'S LIKE TO BE FREE

LORD, HELP ME TO SEE
BEYOND WHAT IS VISIBLE
SHOW ME WHAT YOUR EYES CAN SEE

 LORD HELP ME TO HEAR
 BEYOND WHAT IS AUDIBLE
 HEAR YOUR VOICE SPEAKING TO ME

LORD, USE ME TO TOUCH
WHOMEVER I CAN REACH
TO LET THEM KNOW YOU ARE NEAR

 LORD, USE ME TO SPEAK
 WORDS YOU WANT SPOKEN
 TO IMPART FAITH AND HOPE- NOT FEAR

GOD'S PLAN FOR US

"For I know the plans I have for you," declares the Lord, "plans to prosper you and not to harm you, plans to give you hope and a future." **JER 29:11**

 HOW MUCH LONGER WILL IT TAKE US TO BELIEVE
 THAT THE LORD HAS A PLAN FOR YOU AND FOR ME
 IT INCLUDES HAVING ALL OUR NEEDS MET
 HOW MUCH BETTER DOES IT GET?

35

MY HEART'S DESIRE

TO PLEASE YOU, LORD, IS MY HEARTS' DESIRE
IN ALL WAYS - THOUGHT, WORD, AND DEED
WHOEVER, WHATEVER COMES MY WAY
I WILL FOLLOW YOU - YOU TAKE THE LEAD

PROMPT ME WHAT TO SAY OR DO
TO ENCOURAGE OR TO MEET A NEED
LOVE OTHERS THROUGH ME BECAUSE I BELIEVE
SHOWING LOVE IS LIKE PLANTING A SEED

MAY EACH SEED I PLANT FIND FERTILE SOIL
AND BEAR FRUIT FOR OTHERS TO SHARE
SO MANY WILL COME TO KNOW YOU, LORD
FINDING PEACE AND HOPE - KNOWING YOU CARE

YES, IT'S YOU, LORD, I LIVE TO PLEASE
I HAVE BEEN TRULY BLESSED
I WILL SERVE YOU ALL MY DAYS
WITH ALL THAT'S IN ME - NOTHING LESS

GUARD YOUR MIND

YOUR MIND IS A GARDEN
YOUR THOUGHTS ARE THE SEEDS
THE HARVEST CAN BE EITHER
FLOWERS OR WEEDS   (author unknown)

"And the peace of God, which transcends all understanding, will guard your hearts and your minds in Christ Jesus." Philippians 4

LORD...I PRAY

LORD,

HELP ME TO LOOK BEYOND WHAT I SEE
 IN EACH PERSON THAT I MEET
LET ME SPEAK WORDS OF PEACE AND HOPE
 AND LET YOUR LOVE FLOW THROUGH ME

LORD,

IMPART YOUR WISDOM WHEN I ENCOUNTER
 THOSE TIMES WHEN DECISIONS MATTER
WHEN IT COMES TO CHOOSING MY WAY OR YOURS
 MAY I ALWAYS CHOOSE THE LATTER

LORD,

MAY ALL WHO COME TO KNOW ME FIND ME FAITHFUL
 MAY YOUR LIGHT THAT DWELLS WITHIN ME LEAD THE WAY
MAY MY LIFE LEAD OTHERS TO BELIEVE IN YOU
 MAY THEY SEE THAT I DO JUST AS I SAY

Joseph R. DiCostanzo

MY PRAYER FOR THE USA

LORD, THERE IS THIS SITUATION
THAT IS OF CONCERN TO ME
IT'S ABOUT THIS COUNTRY I LIVE IN
HOME OF THE BRAVE, LAND OF THE FREE

YOU HAVE BLESSED US WITH AN ABUNDANCE
ALL THAT WE NEED AND MORE
YOU ARE THE ONE WE SHOULD HONOR
THE ONE WORTH LIVING FOR

YET WE OFTEN EXPRESS OUR GRATITUDE
TO EVERYONE BUT YOU
ACTING LIKE "IT'S ALL ABOUT ME"
NOT GIVING CREDIT WHERE IT'S DUE

YOU ARE NO LONGER WELCOME
IN A PUBLIC PLACE
SO MANY TAKE YOUR NAME IN VAIN
REALLY? NO LIMIT TO YOUR GRACE?

YOUR WORD IS OFTEN CHALLENGED
REBUKED AND MADE FUN OF
WE HAVE SET EARTHLY STANDARDS
REPLACING YOURS SET FROM ABOVE

WITH ALL THE CHANGES WE HAVE MADE
LIVES HAVE NOT IMPROVED
MORE POVERTY, DIVORCE, FEAR, AND HATE
CHILDREN ABORTED AND MANY ABUSED

INSTEAD OF ADHERING TO YOUR LAWS
WE ARE GIVING EVERYONE CHOICES
INSTEAD OF HEARING WHAT YOU HAVE TO SAY
WE ARE LISTENING TO OTHER VOICES

THERE SEEMS TO BE AN EFFORT
TO DISCREDIT WHAT YOU HAVE SAID
SOME SAY OUR CULTURE IS CHANGING
BELIEVING LIES THEY'VE HEARD AND READ

(continued)

I KNOW THAT YOU ARE SOVEREIGN
NOTHING COMES AS A SURPRISE
YOUR WORD HAS LAID OUT WHAT'S TO COME
AND ITS UNFOLDING BEFORE OUR EYES

IT'S DIFFICULT WATCHING WHAT'S HAPPENING
SO MANY BEING DECEIVED
HELP ME TO STAY WITH YOUR PLAN FOR MY LIFE
HONORING YOU IN THOUGHT, WORD, AND DEED

I PRAY EACH PERSON CALLED BY YOUR NAME
WILL HUMBLE THEMSELVES AND PRAY
THAT THEY SEEK YOUR FACE, CONFESS THEIR SIN,
AND TURN FROM THEIR SINFUL WAYS

I KNOW THIS ISN'T MY PERMANENT HOME
YOU ARE PREPARING A PLACE FOR ME
I PRAY YOU WILL FIND ME FAITHFUL
I LONG TO LIVE WITH YOU ETERNALLY

IN THE MEANTIME, LORD, HELP ME TO BE
YOUR LIGHT IN A PLACE GROWING DIM
IMPART YOUR WISDOM THAT OTHERS MAY SEEK
LIFE, HOPE, AND PEACE WITHIN

HISTORY HAS PROVEN
PROSPERITY IS NO GUARANTEE
HOW MUCH LONGER BEFORE JUDGMENT COMES
TO THE HOME OF THE BRAVE AND THE LAND OF THE FREE

ME – YOUR INSTRUMENT

LORD, HELP ME TO BE AN INSTRUMENT OF YOUR:

LOVE
SHARING YOUR HEART WITH OTHERS AND LEADING THEM TO YOU

PEACE
FOSTERING RECONCILIATION AS AN AMBASSADOR FOR YOU

PRAISE
SINGING, CLAPPING, DANCING, REJOICING IN YOUR PRESENCE

PRAYER
DEDICATING TIME EACH DAY COMMUNICATING WITH YOU

HOPE
REMINDING OTHERS OF YOUR PROMISES AND YOUR PLAN FOR
THEIR LIVES

HEALING
BY THE POWER OF YOUR SPIRIT THAT NOW ABIDES IN ME

WORSHIP
IN SPIRIT AND IN TRUTH ABIDING IN YOUR PRESENCE

LORD, I WANT MY LIFE TO BE
      AN INSTRUMENT IN YOUR SYMPHONY
JOINING THE STRINGS, HARPS AND PIPES
      MUSICAL INSTRUMENTS OF ALL TYPES
ACCOMPANYING THE CHORUS SINGING WITH ONE VOICE
      KING OF KINGS! LORD OF LORDS! REJOICE! REJOICE!

Section 3

Psalms
(Songs of Praise)

Joseph R. DiCostanzo

CHRIST
GOD'S GRACE PERSONIFIED

JESUS, YOU ARE GRACE PERSONIFIED
BORN TO BE CRUCIFIED
A SUBSTITUTE WHO DIED FOR ME
SO FROM GOD'S WRATH I WOULD BE FREE

I'M NOT A SLAVE WHO MUST EARN FAVOR
BUT GOD'S CHILD AND YOU, MY SAVIOR
I'VE BEEN REDEEMED, CLEANSED BY YOUR BLOOD
YOUR GRACE ENGULFS ME LIKE A FLOOD

MY LIFE IS YOURS, AND IT'S MY CHOICE
TO FOLLOW YOU – YIELD TO YOUR VOICE
NO MATTER WHAT MAY COME MY WAY
YOU'LL BE THERE FOR ME EVERY DAY

TRUST HIM… HE LOVES YOU… AS NO ONE ELSE CAN

LORD, I AM YOURS

I THANK YOU, LORD, FOR WHAT YOU'VE DONE
I THANK YOU, LORD, FOR YOU'RE THE ONE
WHO GAVE YOUR LIFE THAT I MIGHT BE
WITH YOU THROUGHOUT ETERNITY

MY REFRAIN:
FROM THIS DAY ON, LORD, I AM YOURS
WITH ALL MY HEART I WORSHIP YOU
I HONOR YOU AND GIVE YOU PRAISE
BE GLORIFIED IN ALL I DO
(YES, LORD, WITH ALL MY HEART I WORSHIP YOU)

EVERY TIME I THINK OF YOU
MY HEART IS FILLED WITH GRATITUDE
THAT YOU DID CARE ENOUGH FOR ME
TO BEAR MY CROSS AND SET ME FREE

I'M NOT THE SAME SINCE I MET YOU
MY LIFE IS CHANGED, MY MIND RENEWED
THINGS THAT ONCE MEANT SO MUCH TO ME
HAVE NO VALUE – YOU'RE ALL I NEED

IT'S BY YOUR SPIRIT I WILL LIVE
YOU LOVE, ENCOURAGE, AND FORGIVE
AND ON THAT DAY I SEE YOUR FACE
I'LL KNOW T'WAS ONLY BY YOUR GRACE

WHAT GOD SEES

I SEE A TINY SEED
YOU SEE A FRUITFUL TREE
YOU DON'T JUST SEE WHAT I SEE
YOU SEE WHAT EACH SEED WILL BE

I SEE A NEW-BORN BABY
YOU SEE A SOUL TO SAVE
YOU DON'T JUST SEE WHAT I SEE
YOU SEE WHAT EACH CHILD CAN BE

I SEE A MAJOR PROBLEM
YOU SEE A TIME FOR ME TO GROW
YOU DON'T JUST SEE WHAT I SEE
YOU SEE WHAT MY FUTURE WILL BE

I SEE A PICTURE OF YOUR SON ON THE CROSS
YOU SEE THE ENEMY DEFEATED
YOU DON'T JUST SEE WHAT I SEE
YOU SEE YOUR CHILDREN COMING HOME

I DON'T SEE ALL YOU SEE
I DON'T KNOW ALL YOU KNOW
BUT WITH YOUR SPIRIT LEADING ME
I'LL ALWAYS KNOW THE WAY TO GO

OUR LORD IS TRULY FAITHFUL

OUR LORD IS TRULY FAITHFUL
HE IS NEAR IN TIME OF NEED
TO OFFER PEACE AND COMFORT
ON OUR BEHALF HE INTERCEDES

OUR LORD IS TRULY FAITHFUL
HE CALMS THE TROUBLED HEART
DON'T WAIT UNTIL YOUR STRENGTH IS SPENT
LOOK TO HIM WHEN TROUBLES START

OUR LORD IS TRULY FAITHFUL
A TRUE AND CONSTANT FRIEND
NOTHING SEPARATES US FROM HIS LOVE
HE'LL BE WITH US 'TIL THE END

OUR LORD IS TRULY FAITHFUL
MERCY AND GRACE IN HIM ABOUND
HE PICKS US UP WHEN WE FALL
AND SETS OUR FEET ON SOLID GROUND

"God is faithful, who has called you into fellowship with his Son, Jesus Christ our Lord." 1Cor. 1:9

""Let us hold unswervingly to the hope we profess, for he who promised is faithful." Heb. 10:23

LORD, IT'S YOU

MY PRECIOUS LORD AND SAVIOR
YOUR SPIRIT OVERWHELMS ME
I'M HUMBLED BY YOUR PRESENCE
ENCOURAGED BY YOUR STEADFAST LOVE

YOU BRING LIGHT INTO MY DARKNESS
YOUR PEACE STILLS MY TROUBLED HEART
YOUR JOY OVERCOMES MY SADNESS
YOU GIVE ME HOPE TO CARRY ON

YOU PAID MY DEBT AND SET ME FREE
IN YOUR NAME I HAVE THE VICTORY
I WALK BY FAITH AND NOT BY SIGHT
KNOWING YOU ARE EVER FAITHFUL

WHEN IT TAKES A MIRACLE

SOME DAYS I ENCOUNTER MORE
THAN I THINK I COULD EVER BEAR
WHEN I SEEK THE HELP OF OTHERS
IT SEEMS THERE IS NO ONE THERE

THEN I REMEMBER I AM NOT ALONE
I HAVE A FRIEND CLOSER THAN A BROTHER
SOMEONE WHO'S ABLE TO PERFORM MIRACLES
AND CAN BE TRUSTED LIKE NO OTHER

HE IMPARTS HIS GRACE AND WISDOM
HIS PATIENCE NEVER WEARS THIN
HIS NAME IS JESUS – TO WHOM I FREELY SUBMIT
MY LORD AND SAVIOR – I OWE MY LIFE TO HIM

Joseph R. DiCostanzo

LORD, I REMEMBER

LORD, I REMEMBER WHEN YOU CAME INTO MY LIFE
ASKED YOU TO BE MY LORD, ACKNOWLEDGED YOUR SACRIFICE
THE DAYS BECAME BRIGHTER, THE BURDENS MUCH LIGHTER
AS I SENSED THE POWER OF YOUR SPIRIT IN ME

I KNOW YOU ARE WITH ME EACH DAY OF MY LIFE
YOUR WORD PROVIDES WISDOM HELPING ME AVOID STRIFE
I NO LONGER SEEK THE APPROVAL OF MAN
BUT ONLY DESIRE TO BE PLEASING TO YOU

I AM GRATEFUL FOR ALL YOU'VE GIVEN TO ME
AN AWESOME HELPMATE, PRECIOUS FRIENDS AND FAMILY
YOU MAKE PROVISIONS TO PROVIDE WHAT WE NEED
AND YOU EVEN FILL THE DESIRES OF MY HEART

I PRAY EACH DAY FOR A NEW REVELATION
A FRESH ANOINTING OF YOUR SPIRIT - NOT A REPUTATION
I WANT TO REMEMBER, BUT NOT DWELL ON THE PAST
SENSE A NEWNESS AND FRESHNESS EACH AND EVERY DAY

MAY I ALWAYS BE WILLING TO FOLLOW YOUR LEAD
SHARE YOUR LOVE WITH OTHERS AND HELP THOSE IN NEED
STAY FOCUSED ON YOU - NOT THE THINGS OF THIS WORLD
WORSHIP AND PRAISE YOU, JESUS, MY LORD

MY LORD, THE OVERCOMER
JOHN 16:33

LORD,
YOU ARE THE OVERCOMER – I AM OVERCOME
BY YOUR PRESENCE, GRACE AND MERCY
YOUR FORGIVENESS AND YOUR LOVE FOR ME

LORD,
YOU ARE THE OVERCOMER – I AM OVERCOME
THINKING OF ALL YOU HAVE DONE FOR ME
THAT I MIGHT LIVE WITH YOU IN ETERNITY

LORD,
YOU ARE THE OVERCOMER – I AM OVERCOME
AS I WATCH THE WAVES BREAKING ON THE SHORE
IT'S YOUR POWER THAT SAYS "GO THIS FAR AND NO MORE"

LORD,
YOU ARE THE OVERCOMER – I AM OVERCOME
KNOWING YOU OVERCAME THE GRAVE
DEATH IS DEFEATED – I AM SAVED!

SECURE IN CHRIST
John 10:28

YOUR POWER IS THE GREATEST
YOUR MERCY SO TENDER
YOUR LOVE IS UNFAILING
I GLADLY SURRENDER

YOUR PATIENCE AMAZING
YOUR GRACE HAS NO MEASURE
YOUR SPIRIT LIVES IN ME
YOUR WORD IS A TREASURE

YOUR WISDOM IS AWESOME
YOUR PROMISES SURE
YOUR PRESENCE IS PRECIOUS
MY FUTURE'S SECURE

Joseph R. DiCostanzo

A TRUE FRIEND
PRO 18:24

<u>**MY REFRAIN:**</u>
THE LORD IS TRULY FAITHFUL   Heb 10:23
A FRIEND WHO WILL NEVER PART   Joshua 1:5
HE STAYS CLOSER THAN A BROTHER   Pro 18:24
GIVES YOU THE DESIRES OF YOUR HEART   Psalm 37:4

HE KNOWS YOUR EVERY WEAKNESS
HE KNOWS ALL YOU'VE DONE WRONG
HE KNOWS YOU MAY IGNORE HIM
YET HE WANTS TO COME ALONG
       YOU SEE, THE LORD IS TRULY FAITHFUL

HE KNOWS WHERE YOU ARE GOING
HE KNOWS WHERE YOU HAVE BEEN
HE KNOWS THAT YOU'VE REJECTED HIM
HURT HIM AGAIN…AND AGAIN
       YET, THE LORD IS TRULY FAITHFUL

WHAT FRIEND CAN YOU TURN TO
WHO STAYS WITH YOU THROUGH IT ALL?
YOU CAN ALWAYS COUNT ON JESUS
TO SUPPORT YOU LEST YOU FALL
       BECAUSE, THE LORD IS TRULY FAITHFUL

CAN YOU EVEN IMAGINE
THAT THERE COULD EVER BE
SOMEONE WHO LOVES YOU JUST AS YOU ARE
AND PROVIDES FOR ALL YOUR NEEDS?
       YES, JESUS IS TRULY FAITHFUL

SOME WHO SAY THAT THEY'RE YOUR FRIEND
MAY END UP BREAKING YOUR HEART
JESUS WILL NEVER LET YOU DOWN
AND CAN MEND YOUR BROKEN HEART
       KNOW THAT JESUS IS TRULY FAITHFUL

EVER MINDFUL

LORD, MAY I ALWAYS BE
MINDFUL OF ALL YOU PROVIDE FOR ME
INSTEAD OF LOOKING FOR SOMETHING MORE
BE GRATEFUL FOR ALL THAT I HAVE

LORD, MAY I ALWAYS BE
MINDFUL YOU ARE CLOSE TO ME
KNOWING WHATEVER COMES MY WAY
YOU ARE THERE TO SEE ME THROUGH

LORD, MAY I ALWAYS BE
MINDFUL YOU HAVE A PLAN FOR ME
SEEK YOUR WISDOM EACH STEP OF THE WAY
HELP ME TO MAKE THE RIGHT CHOICES

LORD, MAY I ALWAYS BE
MINDFUL SALVATION IS NOT FREE
YOU PAID THE PRICE THAT I MIGHT LIVE
FOREVER WITH YOU IN HEAVEN

LORD, MAY I ALWAYS BE
MINDFUL OF YOUR LOVE FOR ME
UNCONDITIONAL LOVE SO UNDESERVING
YOU ARE AN AWESOME GOD

LORD, MAY I ALWAYS BE
MINDFUL LIFE IS A GIFT TO ME
WHEN MY TIME ON EARTH IS OVER
LIFE EVERLASTING WITH YOU BEGINS

PRAISE BE TO YOU, O GOD

PRAISE BE TO YOU, OH GOD ABOVE
FOR YOUR FAITHFULNESS AND UNFAILING LOVE
FOR YOUR SPIRIT WITHIN ME
THAT GIVES NEW LIFE AND SETS ME FREE

PRAISE BE TO YOU, OH GOD MOST HIGH
YOU KNOW MY HEART AND STAY CLOSE BY
YOU KNOW MY THOUGHTS BEFORE I PRAY
AND ALWAYS FORGIVE ME WHEN I STRAY

PRAISE BE TO YOU, OH GOD MY KING
YOU ARE THE REASON THAT I SING
YOUR WORD IS MY SOURCE OF LIGHT
IN YOUR PRESENCE THERE IS NO NIGHT

PRAISE BE TO YOU, OH GOD MY LORD
FOR WISDOM FROM YOUR PRECIOUS WORD
FOR ALL THE BLESSINGS IN MY LIFE
FOR MY CHILDREN AND MY WIFE

<u>MY REFRAIN</u>
PRAISE BE TO YOU, OH GOD OF CREATION
WHO RULES AND REIGNS OVER EVERY NATION
ONE DAY EVERY TONGUE WILL CONFESS
THAT YOU ALONE ARE THE ONE, TRUE GOD

AN EVER-PRESENT HELP

MY REFRAIN:
YOU ARE GREATER THAN I CAN IMAGINE
THERE IS NO ONE WHO COMPARES WITH YOU
YOU'RE ALWAYS THERE TO PICK UP THE PIECES
YOU GIVE ME HOPE AND SEE ME THROUGH

EVEN THROUGH LIFE'S DARKEST MOMENTS
WITH YOUR LIGHT I'M ABLE TO SEE
EVERY TIME I STUMBLE AND FALL
YOUR HAND REACHES OUT TO ME

THOUGH SOME THINGS HAVE OVERWHELMED ME
AND SEEMED TOO HARD TO BEAR
WHEN I'VE CALLED FOR YOU TO HELP ME
YOU HAVE ALWAYS BEEN THERE

THERE ARE TIMES I FIND MYSELF WEARY
STRUGGLING TO FIND MY WAY
BUT WITH YOUR SPIRIT AS MY GUIDE
I CAN MAKE IT THROUGH EACH DAY

YOU'VE INTERVENED MANY TIMES IN MY LIFE
BECAUSE NO OTHER EXPLANATION WILL DO
I CAN ONLY IMAGINE THE NUMBER OF TIMES
MY LIFE HAS BEEN TOUCHED BY YOU!

MY ANCHOR

I LIFT MY EYES TO YOU IN THE HEAVENS
WHERE YOU, MY LORD JESUS, REIGNS
ACKNOWLEDGING YOUR MAJESTY
AND THE POWER IN YOUR PRECIOUS NAME

YOU HAVE LED ME THROUGH TIMES OF DARKNESS
BY REVEALING YOUR MARVELOUS LIGHT
SHOWING ME THE WAY THAT I SHOULD GO
LIKE A BLIND MAN RECEIVING HIS SIGHT

WHEN I HAVE FELT MY STRENGTH WAS SPENT
WITH SO MUCH MORE TO DO
I WAS ABLE TO CARRY ON
WITH THE STRENGTH THAT COMES FROM YOU

WHY YOU CONTINUE TO LOVE ME
I WILL NEVER UNDERSTAND
BUT I'M ETERNALLY GRATEFUL
THAT YOU LOVE ME JUST AS I AM

LORD, YOU HAVE BEEN MY ANCHOR
SO STEADFAST AND SECURE
I AM INDEBTED TO YOU FOR MY EVERY BREATH
MAY YOU FIND ME FAITHFUL AND MY MOTIVES PURE

ABBA FATHER

ABBA FATHER
YOU HAVE BEEN FAITHFUL
THROUGHOUT MY LIFE TIME AND AGAIN

I'M SO GRATEFUL
FOR ALL YOU HAVE DONE
YOU ARE MUCH CLOSER THAN A FRIEND

SO FORGIVING
NO HESITATION
WHEN I REPENT I AM MADE CLEAN

HERE I AM, LORD
WILLING TO SERVE YOU
MAY MY LIFE LEAD OTHERS TO BELIEVE

PRECIOUS FATHER
IF I'M FOUND WORTHY
I WILL OWE IT ALL TO YOUR SON

WHEN THE TIME COMES
THAT MY LIFE HERE ENDS
I PRAY I WILL HEAR THE WORDS "WELL DONE"

TO: JESUS

LORD, YOU'RE THE KEEPER OF MY HEART
THE ONE IN WHOM I PUT MY TRUST
YOUR OMNIPRESENCE GIVES ME PEACE
AND ON YOUR PROMISES I WILL STAND

YOU OFFER SO MUCH, AND I SO LITTLE
I FAIL SO OFTEN, BUT YOU ALWAYS FORGIVE
YOUR GRACE IS GREATER THAN ALL MY TRANSGRESSIONS
SO GREAT A LOVE I CAN'T COMPREHEND

YOUR NAME'S LIKE AN OINTMENT THAT TAKES AWAY PAIN
QUIETS MY SPIRIT LIKE A SPRING RAIN
YOUR NAME IS A RAY OF LIGHT IN A DARK PLACE
IT'S NO WONDER MY HOPE IS IN YOU

AWESOME, MAJESTIC KING OF ALL KINGS
REDEEMER, PROVIDER WHO MAKES MY HEART SING
SAVIOR, DELIVERER, MY CLOSEST FRIEND
YOU ARE THE ULTIMATE – THE BEGINNING AND THE END!

ONCE FOR ALL

ONCE FOR ALL CHRIST TOOK UP HIS CROSS
ENDURING THE PAIN AND AGONY
BEARING OUR SHAME THAT PRECEDED HIS DEATH
SECURING FOR US AN ETERNITY

BECAUSE OF CHRIST'S PERFECT SACRIFICE
THE POWER OF DEATH IS DEFEATED
NOW NOTHING IS OUT OF HIS CONTROL
HIS SACRIFICE NEED NOT BE REPEATED

ONCE FOR ALL - IT WAS HIS CHOICE
ALL HE REQUIRES IS THAT WE BELIEVE
THEN WE CAN APPROACH HIM WITH CONFIDENCE
KNOWING WHAT HE HAS PROMISED WE WILL RECEIVE

YOU (LORD) ARE...

YOU ARE THE CREATOR
  OF HEAVEN AND EARTH
YOU CREATED ALL MANKIND
  FROM CONCEPTION TO BIRTH

YOU ARE THE SHEPHERD
  WHO TENDS TO HIS SHEEP
THE PROVIDER AND PROTECTOR
  OF THOSE WHO ARE WEAK

YOU ARE THE KING OF KINGS
  WHO SITS ON THE THRONE
WE ARE YOUR SUBJECTS
  WHO WORSHIP YOU ALONE

YOU ARE THE POTTER
  WE ARE THE CLAY
SHAPE US TO BE VESSELS
  THAT SERVE YOU EACH DAY

GOD PROMPTS ME...

IT'S NOT WHAT YOU'VE READ,
  BUT WHAT I'VE SAID.
DON'T PROCEED
  APART FROM ME.
TAKE TIME TO ASK
  BEFORE EACH TASK.
MY PROMISE TO YOU
  TO BE FAITHFUL AND TRUE.

Joseph R. DiCostanzo

Section 4

Personal Reflections

Joseph R. DiCostanzo

THE SUN:

* RISES

* A LIGHT IN THE WORLD

* WARMS THE BODY

* A PART OF OUR UNIVERSE

* SETS

* REVOLVES

* DAYS ARE NUMBERED

* BALL OF FIRE

* IN THE HEAVENLIES

* CASTS SHADOWS

 * NEEDED FOR LIFE

THE SON:

* IS RISEN

* THE LIGHT OF THE WORLD

* WARMS THE SOUL

* CREATED OUR UNIVERSE

* CONSTANT SOURCE OF
  LIGHT

* STEADFAST

* EVERLASTING

* ALL-CONSUMING FIRE

* IN HEAVEN

* HAS NO SHADOW

* NEEDED FOR LIFE
  EVERLASTING

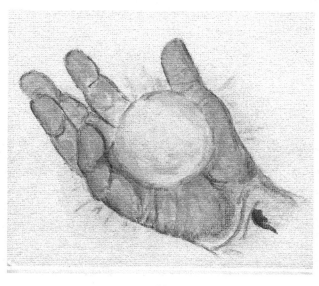

Joseph R. DiCostanzo

THE SURVIVOR
HONORING THE "LOST BOYS" OF SUDAN

RECALLING THE CHALLENGES FROM PAST TO PRESENT
TEARS CAUSE THE EYES TO SWELL
BUT IN THE HEART AND MIND OF THE SURVIVOR
HOPE IS ALIVE AND WELL

THE QUESTION ISN'T WHY IT ALL HAPPENED
BUT WHERE DO WE GO FROM HERE
THE FUTURE IS WHAT REALLY MATTERS
THE PAST IS SOMETHING HELD DEAR

THE LIGHT IN THE EYES OF THE SURVIVOR
SHINES SO THAT ALL MAY SEE
THE PATH TO THE FUTURE BEGINS IN THE PRESENT
AND WHERE WE GO GOD WILL BE

THE SMILE ON THE FACE OF THE SURVIVOR
NEEDS NO WORDS TO IMPART
WITH CHRIST IN YOUR LIFE, THOUGH YOU FACE THE IMPOSSIBLE
HIS JOY REMAINS IN YOUR HEART

IF YOU WANT TO BE A SURVIVOR
THEN BE WILLING TO ALWAYS FORGIVE
JESUS IS THE SOURCE OF OUR LIGHT AND SMILE
HE IS THE REASON WE LIVE

THE GIFT OF LIFE (ONE MORE DAY)...PS. 118:24

I RECEIVED A GIFT TODAY
WHICH SURPASSED MY EXPECTATIONS
IT FILLED MY MIND WITH MEMORIES
THAT MY HEART WILL ALWAYS TREASURE

ONE MORE DAY TO SHARE WITH MY WIFE
AND TELL HER THAT I LOVE HER
ONE MORE DAY FOR A SWEET EMBRACE
AND TO GIVE ALL I HAVE TO OFFER

ONE MORE DAY TO TELL OUR CHILDREN
MY LOVE FOR THEM WILL NEVER END
ONE MORE DAY TO LET THEM KNOW
I WILL ALWAYS BE THEIR FRIEND

ONE MORE DAY TO STAND BESIDE
SOMEONE WHO IS ALONE
ONE MORE DAY TO OFFER HOPE
WHEN ONE FEELS THEY'RE ON THEIR OWN

ONE MORE DAY TO RISE AND SHINE
AND GIVE GOD ALL THE GLORY
ONE MORE DAY TO SING GOD'S PRAISES
RATHER THAN FRET AND WORRY

ONE MORE DAY TO SHARE GOD'S LOVE
AND TELL OTHERS OF HIS PLAN
ONE MORE DAY, ONE MORE CHANCE
TO WITNESS TO ALL I CAN

ONE MORE DAY TO PRAY FOR OTHERS
AND GIVE THEM A REASON TO SMILE
ONE MORE DAY TO MAKE "WRONGS" "RIGHT"
AND TO GO THE EXTRA MILE

ONE MORE DAY TO READ GOD'S WORD
AND THANK HIM FOR HIS GRACE
ONE MORE DAY TO ENJOY HIS PEACE
'TIL I MEET HIM FACE-TO-FACE

THANK YOU, LORD, FOR ONE MORE DAY
WHERE ALL MY NEEDS ARE MET
MY LOVE FOR YOU WILL NEVER END
YOUR FAITHFULNESS I'LL NOT FORGET

Joseph R. DiCostanzo

REFLECTIONS (1)

A SUNNY DAY	A MOTHER'S TOUCH
AN OCEAN BREEZE	A WARM EMBRACE
A CLOUDLESS SKY	A LOVING HEART
A FEELING FREE	A SMILING FACE
A CHILD IS BORN	A FATHER'S HEART
AN AWESOME SIGHT	A DAD WHO"S THERE
A LOT OF WORK	AN OPEN HAND
A TRUE DELIGHT	A FRIEND WHO CARES
A BABY'S CRY	A SUNNY SKY
A NEWBORN'S COO	AN OCEAN SHORE
A ROCKING CHAIR	A GENTLE BREEZE
A PEEK-A-BOO	A KITE THAT SOARS
A SUMMER SKY	A TALL OAK TREE
A BIRD FLIES FREE	AN AWESOME SIGHT
A ROBIN'S SONG	A FALL WONDER
A SWEET MELODY	A CRISP, COOL NIGHT

REFLECTIONS (2)

A SIN OF MAN	A FAITHFUL WIFE
A GOD WHO GAVE	A CARING FRIEND
A SON WHO CAME	A HELP MATE TOO
A LIFE TO SAVE	A TRUE GOD SEND
A GRIEVING HEART	A JOYFUL HEART
A FEARFUL DAY	A PEACEFUL DAY
AN OUTSTRETCHED HAND	A SONG OF JOY
A TIME TO PRAY	A TIME TO PRAISE
A TROUBLED SOUL	A SOLEMN VOW
A FRIEND IN NEED	A TRUE ROMANCE
A RAY OF HOPE	A WEDDING RING
A FRIEND INDEED	A TIME TO DANCE
A SHATTERED DREAM	A FROZEN LAKE
A BROKEN HEART	A SOFT, CLEAN SNOW
A NEW DAY DAWNS	A GLISTENIMG TREE
A BRAND-NEW START	A WINTER SHOW

JESUS...HE...

JESUS SEES BEYOND WHAT'S VISIBLE
HE REACHES WHERE NO ONE ELSE CAN
JESUS SPEAKS WITHOUT SAYING A WORD
BECAUSE HE IS BOTH GOD AND MAN

JESUS WILL LEAD WHEN YOU STEP ASIDE
HE WILL FORGIVE WHEN YOU REPENT
JESUS LOVES YOU WITHOUT A DOUBT
WAVERS NOT FROM HIS COVENANT

JESUS IS A TRUSTWORTHY FRIEND
HE'S FAITHFUL TO DO AS HE SAYS
JESUS KNOWS THE INTENT OF YOUR HEART
HE KNOWS THE NUMBER OF YOUR DAYS

JESUS GIVES STRENGTH WHEN YOU ARE WEAK
HE'S THE PROVIDER OF ALL YOU NEED
JESUS IS AN EVER-PRESENT FRIEND
HIS PROMISES ARE GUARANTEED

JESUS IS WAITING FOR YOU TO CALL
HE'S ALWAYS NEAR – NEVER FAR
JESUS HAS A PLAN FOR YOUR LIFE
HE INVITES YOU JUST AS YOU ARE

ANGELS?

I THINK OF PEOPLE, SOME I HAVE NEVER MET
WHO HAVE HELPED ME IN WAYS I WON'T SOON FORGET
SOME NEVER BOTHERED TO GIVE ME THEIR NAME
BUT I AM FOREVER GRATEFUL JUST THE SAME

MY REFRAIN:
GOD'S ANGELS ARE WATCHING OVER ME
OF THIS I AM SURE AS I CAN BE
HE HAS BEEN FAITHFUL TO SEE ME THROUGH
EVEN WHEN I WAS NOT AWARE I NEEDED HIM TO

I STILL REMEMBER THE NIGHT WE WERE WED
WE STOPPED FOR GAS AND THE BATTERY WENT DEAD
SOME YOUNG MEN CAME BY WITH OUR CAR HOOD AJAR
THEY USED THEIR BATTERY TO START OUR CAR

WE ARRIVED IN CALIFORNIA WITH NO PLACE TO LIVE
THE LORD SENT A YOUNG MAN WITH FREE TIME TO GIVE
HE PATIENTLY DROVE US TO SEARCH FOR A PLACE
AND HELPED US TO SOLVE A CONCERN THAT WE FACED

MORE THAN ONCE MY CREDIT CARD WAS LOST
WHICH CAUSED GRIEF AND CONCERN ABOUT THE COST
EACH TIME IT WAS TURNED IN TO A PERSON IN CHARGE
I AM GRATEFUL TO THOSE WHO RETURNED THE LOST CARD

CAN YOU THINK OF ANY TIMES IN YOUR PAST
SOMEONE, UNKNOWN BY YOU, INTERVENED ON YOUR BEHALF?
CAME OUT OF NOWHERE, SPOKE WORDS YOU NEEDED TO HEAR?
WAS IT ALL HAPPENSTANCE, OR PROOF THAT OUR GOD IS NEAR?

For He will command His angels concerning you to guard you in all your ways;
they will lift you up in their hands, so that you will not strike your foot against a
stone. Psalm 91:11-12

Joseph R. DiCostanzo

ARE YOU FOR REAL?

SO MANY PEOPLE ASSUME A ROLE
PERFORMING AS THOUGH THEY'RE A STAR
ACTING, MIMICKING, PLAYING A PART FOR SO LONG
THEY FORGET WHO THEY REALLY ARE

ARE YOU FOR REAL?
IS WHAT I SEE TRULY WHO YOU ARE?
OR IS WHAT I SEE LIKE A MANEQUIN
IN THE WINDOW OF A STORE?

ARE YOU FOR REAL?
IS WHAT YOU SAY TRULY HOW YOU FEEL?
OR IS WHAT YOU SAY AN OPPORTUNITY
TO SWAY, DECEIVE OR THRILL?

ARE YOU FOR REAL?
IS WHAT YOU DO DONE FROM THE HEART?
OR ARE YOU JUST FOLLOWING OTHERS
ACTING THEIR ROLE – NOT PLAYING YOUR PART?

ARE YOU FOR REAL?
IS WHAT YOU BELIEVE EVIDENT TO ALL YOU MEET?
OR BY YOUR RESPONSE, OR LACK THEREOF,
DO YOUR CONVICTIONS REMAIN DISCREET?

BY BEING JUST ONE PERSON
UNDIVIDED AND COMPLETE`
YOU'LL BE KNOWN FOR YOUR INTEGRITY
RESPECTED BY ALL THOSE YOU MEET

"You are the salt of the earth. But if the salt loses its saltiness, how can it be made salty again? It is no longer good for anything, except to be thrown out and trampled underfoot." Mat. 5:13

LIFE'S PATH
(OUR JOURNEY)

Life takes each of us on a path to we don't know where. **(Isa 42:16)** **(Pro 4:25-27)** But, if we stay in the light **(Jn 8:12)** there is nothing to fear. **(Isa 41:10)** Our life's path will be filled with pleasantness and uncertainties. But, God promises to be there for us. **(Ps 46:1)**

Others may join us for a time, but there is only one who will travel the exact path with us all the way. **(Josh 1:5)** Every experience and encounter with others will play a role in molding us into the person we are becoming. **(Isa 64:8)**

Others are not responsible for who we become. We are. The way we respond to each experience and relationship will ultimately determine the attitude and wisdom we carry with us through life. **(Pro 3:13)**

To a great extent where our path leads is up to us. We may need to alter our course at times. We will face challenges along the way, but don't let them stop us for long - or continue to dwell on them - or we will end up stuck there for a very long time.

Each challenge is not an obstacle, but an opportunity to:
(a) increase in knowledge and wisdom and/or **(James 1:5)**
(b) use the knowledge and wisdom we have gained and/or
(c) solicit assistance from those who have more knowledge and wisdom than we do.

Rest assured there is a unique plan and purpose for each of our lives. **(Jer 29:11)** We should continually be developing the talents with which we have been gifted. Our greatest fulfillment is realized when we use our talents for the benefit of others. **(1Pet 4:10)**

(continued)

We may entertain the thought, "I did not ask to be born so I am indebted to no one".

If this is what we think, then we are only revealing our selfish nature. This line of thought only causes grief, loneliness and disappointment. We may want to hold others responsible for where our life has taken us. Although others may be the source of some of our experiences and/or frustrations, we are the ones who determine how we will use those experiences and frustrations to prepare us for the rest of our journey.

Perhaps we forgot that expression "when life serves you lemons - make lemonade". Consider the idea that we could share the lemonade with those who may not have lemons, or have not yet learned how to make lemonade. We should not be selective when sharing our lemonade. Even those who have hurt us, used us, disappointed us or put obstacles in our path get thirsty. The lemonade may "quench" that which keeps us apart. (Matt 5:44)

We may have thought, "the path I want to take has been blocked, and nothing will clear the way". Consider the possibility that there may not be a path in the direction we are heading (**Pro 3:6**), or the path has an obstacle that requires more than we are prepared to handle.

There is nothing wrong with taking a detour to circumvent the obstacle and continue on our way. Opportunities for personal growth and learning often present themselves as a challenge. Even a failed attempt is a success if we learn from the experience. It is critical that we do not lose hope, or concern ourselves with what tomorrow may bring. (**Matt 6:34**) As we forge the unique path in our life, we must maintain a sense of humor so we will be able to laugh at ourselves and laugh with others. (**Pro 17:22**)

(continued)

We will have needs, but must not dwell on what we are lacking - rather be grateful for what we do have. Consider giving out of our need. (**Pro 11:24**) If we need a hug - give a hug. If we need a friend - be a friend. Whatever we are lacking - consider giving what we are able to others who are even less fortunate.

We live each day to do just as we would. We can do what some call "bad" or do what is good. (**Eph 2:10**) We can make someone happy (**Eph 4:29**), or make someone sad. What will we do with each day that we have? (**Matt 12:36**) We can pick someone up (**1Thes 5:11**) or put someone down. We can offer a smile or show them a frown. We may not always realize the impact we are having on the lives of others who are forging their own paths. (**Lk 7:23**)

It is just as important to be aware of the impact we allow others to have on our lives. As much as we may want to believe we can make it on our own, we can't. We need others. (**1Cor 12:14,19,20**) and, yes, others need us. We should not think that we are better than others (**1Pet 5:6**) - we are not. (**1Cor 1:31**) But give them reason for them to think that of us. (**Phil 2:3-7**)

We are leaving a trail behind us as we journey through life. What are we planting along the way? Will others be blessed by the fruit of our labor when they cross our path? We must remember to stop, rest and enjoy where we are on our path. Take time to plant roses, smell roses and give roses. Make others feel special - because they are - and so are we!

When all is said and done, and we have come to the end of our earthly journey, we will meet the one and only one who has accompanied us throughout our journey in life. If it is determined that our name appears in "**the**" Book (**Rev 3:5**), our Lord will welcome us into the place he has prepared for us. (**Jn 14:2-3**) If our name does not appear in "**the**" Book, we will regret it forever.

Joseph R. DiCostanzo

PEACE AND CONTENTMENT

AM I CONTENT WITH MY NEEDS MET?
NO, I WANT MORE, BUT WHAT FOR
THE MORE I HAVE, THE MORE I DESIRE
AND PEACE AND CONTENTMENT ESCAPE ME

AM I CONTENT WHEN I EARN MORE?
NO, LIKE A FIRE THAT'S NEVER QUENCHED
THE MORE I HAVE, THE MORE I SPEND
AND PEACE AND CONTENTMENT ESCAPE ME

AM I CONTENT AND FEELING SECURE
LIVING A LIFE WITH FEW CONCERNS?
NO, THE MORE I HAVE, THE MORE I WORRY
AND PEACE AND CONTENTMENT ESCAPE ME

AM I CONTENT WITH ALL THESE "THINGS"
I'VE ACCUMULATED ALL MY LIFE?
NO, ONE DAY I'LL LEAVE IT ALL BEHIND
AND PEACE AND CONTENTMENT ESCAPE ME

LORD, FORGIVE ME FOR NOT BEING GRATEFUL
AND ALWAYS DESIRING MORE
IT'S IN YOU I FIND PEACE AND CONTENTMENT
YOU ARE THE ONE I AM LIVING FOR

APPEARANCE -VS- REALITY

WHAT I SEE IS NOT ALWAYS WHAT IT APPEARS TO BE – NO MORE THAN THE WAY I LOOK REFLECTS WHO I REALLY AM. IF THE LORD SAYS HE DOES NOT LOOK ON THE OUTWARD APPEARANCE, (1SAMUEL 16:7), WHO AM I TO MAKE ASSUMPTIONS OR PASS JUDGMENT BASED ON APPEARANCES?

WHAT I DO KNOW IS THAT I MUST BE MORE CONCERNED ABOUT THE PART OF ME THAT IS MOST IMPORTANT TO MY LORD AND SAVIOR – MY HEART! MY HEART REVEALS TO THE LORD WHO THE REAL ME IS. NOT WHAT I SEE IN THE MIRROR, AND NOT WHAT OTHERS MAY THINK OF ME.

HE IS THE ONLY ONE I NEED TO PLEASE IN THOUGHT, WORD AND DEED. HE KNOWS MY MOTIVES. MY PRAYER IS:
PSALM 51:10 "CREATE IN ME A CLEAN HEART AND RENEW A STEADFAST SPIRIT WITHIN ME."

I DESIRE TO BE WHERE GOD WANTS ME TO BE, AND DOING WHAT HE WANTS ME TO DO. PLEASING MY LORD GOES BEYOND JUST KNOWING ABOUT HIM. IT'S MORE AND THAN JUST TELLING OTHERS ABOUT HIM. IT'S ABOUT HAVING AN INTIMATE RELATIONSHIP WITH HIM.

OTHERS GET TO KNOW THE REAL ME WITHOUT MY SAYING A WORD. OTHERS WILL KNOW I AM A CHRISTIAN BY MY LOVE; WHAT I SAY AND HOW I SAY IT; WHAT I DO AND HOW I DO IT; HOW I RESPOND TO SITUATIONS AND INDIVIDUALS NO MATTER WHAT THE CIRCUMSTANCES.

I MUST NOT LET MY THOUGHTS, FEELINGS OR APPEARANCE BE INFLUENCED BY STANDARDS SET BY ANY OTHER THAN MY LORD AND SAVIOR, JESUS CHRIST.

"For this reason, since the day we heard about you, we have not stopped praying for you. We continually ask God to fill you with the knowledge of his will through all the wisdom and understanding that the Spirit gives, so that you may live a life worthy of the Lord and please him in every good, growing in the knowledge of God." Col 1:9-10

"TRUST ME"

WHEN THE GOING GETS TOUGH
AND ALL I DO ISN'T ENOUGH
I CAN HEAR JESUS SAYING,
"TRUST ME"

AT THE END OF MY "ROPE"
WITH NOT AN OUNCE OF HOPE
I CAN HEAR JESUS SAYING
"TRUST ME"

WHEN MY LIFE SEEMS A MESS
FULL OF STRIFE AND STRESS
I CAN HEAR JESUS SAYING
"TRUST ME"

WHEN PEACE ESCAPES ME
AND LIFE IS A FRENZY
I CAN HEAR JESUS SAYING
"TRUST ME"

WITH DECISIONS TO MAKE
NOT KNOWING WHICH PATH TO TAKE
I CAN HEAR JESUS SAYING
"TRUST ME"

YES, LORD, I WILL TRUST YOU
THERE'S NO ONE I CAN TURN TO
WHO HAS BEEN SO FAITHFUL AND TRUE

THROUGH THE EASY AND TOUGH TIMES
I PREFER TO DO NOTHING
WITHOUT FIRST CHECKING WITH YOU

THROUGH IT ALL

THROUGH IT ALL, LORD, YOU'VE BEEN THERE
EVERY TIME AND EVERYWHERE
YOU'VE BEEN MY ROCK, A SURE FOUNDATION
DESERVING OF ALL ADORATION

MAY MY WORDS BE ALWAYS TRUE
ENCOURAGING OTHERS TO FOLLOW YOU
YOU PIERCE THE DARKNESS WITH YOUR LIGHT
YOUR FAITHFUL PRESENCE DISPELS THE NIGHT

BE MY PARTNER IN ALL I DO
GIVE ME WISDOM TO SEE THINGS THROUGH
SHOW ME WHAT YOU WANT DONE
THAT I MAY GLORIFY YOUR SON

MEDITATION: PROVERBS 3:6

FATHER, MY PATHS HAVE OFTEN SEEMED CROOKED AND
OBSTRUCTED. AT TIMES IT SEEMED THERE WAS NO PATH AT ALL. I
WAS NOT ALWAYS QUICK TO ACKNOWLEDGE YOU, BUT, AS YOU
PROMISED, WHEN I DID, YOU ALWAYS MADE A WAY, CLEARED
THE WAY, AND/OR LEAD THE WAY! YOU ARE THE WAY!

MEDITATION: ISAIAH 41:10

FATHER, YOUR LOVE DISPELS MY FEARS AND ENCOURAGES ME. I
ACKNOWLEDGE YOU AS THE SOURCE OF MY STRENGTH AND MY
UNSEEN HELP. YOU HAVE BEEN EVER PRESENT AND FAITHFUL TO
UPHOLD ME DURING THOSE MANY OCCASIONS WHEN I WOULD
HAVE FALLEN. FOR YOUR FAITHFULNESS, I AM FOREVER
GRATEFUL.

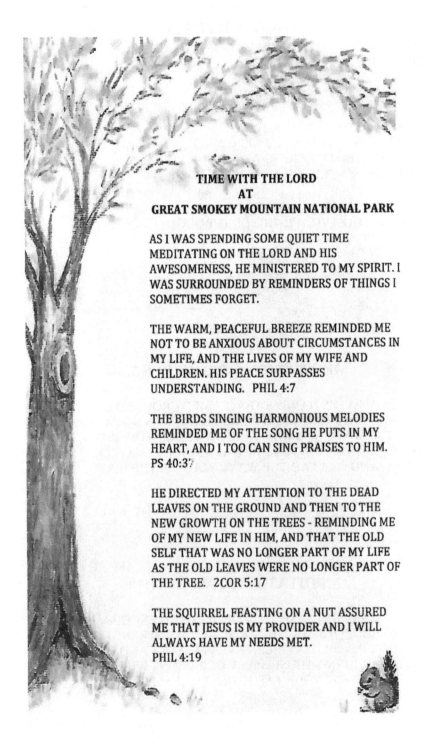

Joseph R. DiCostanzo

TIME WITH THE LORD
AT
GREAT SMOKEY MOUNTAIN NATIONAL PARK

AS I WAS SPENDING SOME QUIET TIME
MEDITATING ON THE LORD AND HIS
AWESOMENESS, HE MINISTERED TO MY SPIRIT. I
WAS SURROUNDED BY REMINDERS OF THINGS I
SOMETIMES FORGET.

THE WARM, PEACEFUL BREEZE REMINDED ME
NOT TO BE ANXIOUS ABOUT CIRCUMSTANCES IN
MY LIFE, AND THE LIVES OF MY WIFE AND
CHILDREN. HIS PEACE SURPASSES
UNDERSTANDING. PHIL 4:7

THE BIRDS SINGING HARMONIOUS MELODIES
REMINDED ME OF THE SONG HE PUTS IN MY
HEART, AND I TOO CAN SING PRAISES TO HIM.
PS 40:3

HE DIRECTED MY ATTENTION TO THE DEAD
LEAVES ON THE GROUND AND THEN TO THE
NEW GROWTH ON THE TREES - REMINDING ME
OF MY NEW LIFE IN HIM, AND THAT THE OLD
SELF THAT WAS NO LONGER PART OF MY LIFE
AS THE OLD LEAVES WERE NO LONGER PART OF
THE TREE. 2COR 5:17

THE SQUIRREL FEASTING ON A NUT ASSURED
ME THAT JESUS IS MY PROVIDER AND I WILL
ALWAYS HAVE MY NEEDS MET.
PHIL 4:19

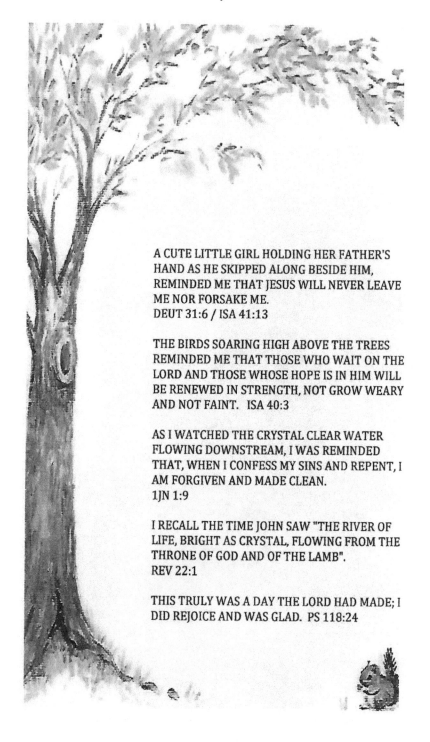

A CUTE LITTLE GIRL HOLDING HER FATHER'S
HAND AS HE SKIPPED ALONG BESIDE HIM,
REMINDED ME THAT JESUS WILL NEVER LEAVE
ME NOR FORSAKE ME.
DEUT 31:6 / ISA 41:13

THE BIRDS SOARING HIGH ABOVE THE TREES
REMINDED ME THAT THOSE WHO WAIT ON THE
LORD AND THOSE WHOSE HOPE IS IN HIM WILL
BE RENEWED IN STRENGTH, NOT GROW WEARY
AND NOT FAINT. ISA 40:3

AS I WATCHED THE CRYSTAL CLEAR WATER
FLOWING DOWNSTREAM, I WAS REMINDED
THAT, WHEN I CONFESS MY SINS AND REPENT, I
AM FORGIVEN AND MADE CLEAN.
1JN 1:9

I RECALL THE TIME JOHN SAW "THE RIVER OF
LIFE, BRIGHT AS CRYSTAL, FLOWING FROM THE
THRONE OF GOD AND OF THE LAMB".
REV 22:1

THIS TRULY WAS A DAY THE LORD HAD MADE; I
DID REJOICE AND WAS GLAD. PS 118:24

Joseph R. DiCostanzo

Section 5

Inspirations From God and His Word

GOD SPEAKS...

OKAY, SO YOU'RE FEELING A LITTLE BIT OVERWHELMED.

COULD IT BE BECAUSE YOU ARE TRYING TO ACCOMPLISH THINGS WITHOUT ME?

YOU ARE IN A POSITION THAT YOU WERE NEVER MEANT TO HANDLE ON YOUR OWN. IT IS NOT MY PLAN TO BURDEN YOU, BUT TO INVITE YOU TO BE A PART OF MY PLAN.

YOUR FAITHFULNESS HAS PROVEN TO ME THAT I CAN ACCOMPLISH GREAT THINGS THROUGH YOU. CONTINUE TO SEEK ME, WAIT ON ME, FOLLOW MY LEAD - DON'T RUN AHEAD OF ME.

CONTINUE TO ALLOW MY LOVE TO FLOW THROUGH YOU, AND IN MY TIME YOU WILL SEE THE FRUITS OF YOUR LABOR.

BE ENCOURAGED.
BE PATIENT.
BE STILL.

I AM AN OVERCOMER

EPHESUS (REV 2:1-7)
NOT ONLY DID JESUS CHRIST TRADE PLACES WITH ME
BY SUFFERING AND DYING ON CALVARY'S TREE
HE INVITED ME TO EAT FROM HEAVEN'S LIFE TREE
IN THE PARADISE OF GOD FOR ETERNITY

SMYRNA (REV 2:8-11)
THOUGH THIS LIFE MAY BE TOUGH AND MAY EVEN BRING PAIN
HE PROMISED ONLY ONE DEATH FOR ALL THOSE WHO REMAIN...
FAITHFUL TO HIM THROUGH ALL TRIBULATION
AN EVERLASTING LIFE IN A HEAVENLY NATION

PERGAMUS (REV 2:12-17)
YOU GAVE ME A WHITE STONE AND SAID "YOU'RE NOW FREE"
I GIVE YOU A NEW NAME, AND MANNA TO EAT
OLD THINGS ARE PASSED AWAY, NOW ALL THINGS ARE NEW
AND WHEREVER YOU GO CHILD I'LL BE THERE WITH YOU

THYATIRA (REV 2:18-29)
BEING FAITHFUL TO HIM AND NOT DRIFTING AFAR
DARKNESS IS OVERCOME BY THE DAWN'S MORNING STAR
WHEN FACED WITH GREAT DANGER, YOU NEED NOT COWER
FOR HE'S PROMISED US HIS OVERCOMING POWER

SARDIS (REV 3:1-6)
STAYING STRONG, ALERT AND WATCHFUL THROUGH THE NIGHT
I WALK WITH MY LORD IN GARMENTS OF WHITE
HIS PROMISE IS TO ME AND TO ALL WHO STAND FAST
OUR NAME IS IN THE BOOK OF LIFE, HE'S FORGIVEN THE PAST

PHILADELPHIA (REV 3:7-13)
I WON'T DENY YOU, LORD, YOU HAVE OPENED THE DOOR
YOU'VE PROMISED YOUR FAITHFUL A CROWN AND MUCH MORE
DURING TIMES OF TRIAL WHEN I'M PUT TO THE TEST
I'LL EXULT YOUR NAME, O GOD, AND ENJOY PEACE AND REST

LAODICEA (REV 3:14-22)
THERE IS NO EARTHLY THING I TRULY DESIRE
ONLY WHAT YOU OFFER, LORD, REFINED IN THE FIRE
I WANT TO HEAR YOUR VOICE, AND YOURS ALONE
AND IN MY WHITE GARMENTS WORSHIP YOU ON YOUR THRONE

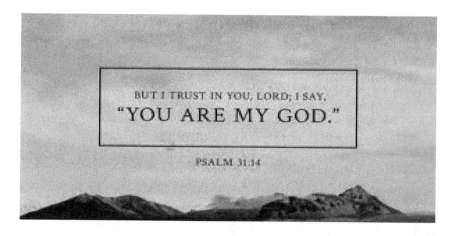

INSPIRATION FROM PSALM 31

IN YOU, O LORD, I TAKE REFUGE
FROM THE MANY THINGS I FACE
IN YOU, O LORD, I TAKE REFUGE
SEEKING YOUR WISDOM AND YOUR GRACE

IN YOU, O LORD, I AM NOT ASHAMED
TO PROCLAIM YOU AS SAVIOR AND LORD
IN YOU, O LORD, I AM NOT ASHAMED
TO DECLARE YOUR WORD IS MY SWORD

IN YOU, O LORD, I FIND PERFECT PEACE
WHEN EVENTS IN MY LIFE CAUSE DISTRESS
IN YOU, O LORD, I FIND PERFECT PEACE
FOR IN YOUR PRESENCE I CAN REST

IN YOU, O LORD, IS MY STRENGTH FOR TODAY
YOU ARE MY ROCK AND MY FORTRESS
IN YOU, O LORD, IS MY STRENGTH FOR TODAY
BECAUSE IN YOU NOTHING IS HOPELESS

IN YOU, O LORD, I AM HUMBLED
THINKING OF ALL YOU'VE DONE FOR ME
IN YOU, O LORD, I AM HUMBLED
YOU HAVE BLESSED ME ABUNDANTLY

Joseph R. DiCostanzo

GOD'S WORD/ GOD'S PLAN

I READ OF GOD'S CREATION
OF ADAM AND OF EVE
OF HOW THEY LIVED IN PARADISE
AND HOW THEY WERE DECEIVED

      DOING WHAT WAS FORBIDDEN
      NOT HEEDING WHAT GOD DID SAY
      IF WE DESIRE TO FOLLOW GOD'S PLAN
      IT'S GOD'S WORD WE MUST OBEY

ON EARTH GOD SAW MUCH WICKEDNESS
HIS HEART WAS FILLED WITH PAIN
HE FOUND RIGHTEOUSNESS IN NOAH
AND WARNED HIM OF THE RAIN

      GOD TOLD NOAH TO BUILD AN ARK
      TO SAVE HIM AND HIS FAMILY
      FROM A FLOOD THAT WOULD COVER THE EARTH
      TO CLEANSE IT OF INIQUITY

IN ABRAHAM GOD FOUND A MAN
WILLING TO LEAVE ALL BEHIND
AND FOLLOW GOD'S INSTRUCTIONS
BY FAITH... WITH AN OPEN MIND

      SO ABRAHAM WAS GIVEN MORE
      THAN ALL HE LEFT BEHIND
      A GREAT NATION, LAND AND A COVENANT
      MANY BLESSINGS OF EVERY KIND

GOD'S COVENANT WITH ABRAHAM
DID NOT END WHEN HE DIED
ISAAC INHERITED GOD'S PROMISE
AND JACOB WOULD NOT BE DENIED

      ISAAC LIED ABOUT HIS WIFE
      AND JACOB TRICKED HIS FATHER
      SOME THINGS JUST DON'T SEEM RIGHT
      BUT GOD'S PLANS MAN CANNOT ALTER

(continued)

THEN THERE WAS JACOB'S SON, JOSEPH
WITH HIS COAT OF MANY COLORS
WHO SHARED A DREAM THAT HE HAD
AND DREW THE WRATH OF HIS BROTHERS

    BUT GOD HAD A PLAN FOR JOSEPH
    HE INTERPRETED PHARAOH'S DREAMS
    AND WAS REWARDED MUCH POWER IN EGYPT
    AND HELD IN HIGH ESTEEM

GOD ALSO HAD A PLAN FOR MOSES
HE SPARED HIS LIFE AS A CHILD
GOD SENT HIM TO SPEAK TO PHARAOH
WHO SOON BECAME VERY RILED

    MOSES LED GOD'S PEOPLE FOR 40 YEARS
    THROUGH THE DESERT TO THE PROMISED LAND
    GOD SENT A CLOUD BY DAY AND FIRE BY NIGHT
    AND AFFIRMED ON HIS WORD WE CAN STAND

I MARVEL AT THE MAN CALLED DAVID
NO FEAR OF LIONS, GIANTS, OR MAN
AND WHEN HE SAW BATHSHEBA
SHOULD HAVE RUN "AS FAST AS HE CAN"

    GOD MADE A COVENANT WITH DAVID
    THRU HIM GOD WOULD ESTABLISH HIS THRONE
    THE LINEAGE OF THE KING OF KINGS
    WOULD BE THROUGH DAVID'S SEED ALONE

GOD REVEALED HIMSELF THROUGH HIS PROPHETS
HE SHARED WHAT WAS ON HIS HEART
SEEKING REPENTANCE AND GIVING HOPE
AND LOVING COUNSEL TO IMPART

    SOMETIMES GOD'S MESSAGE WAS HEEDED
    SOMETIMES IT FELL ON DEAF EARS
    THE LESSON TO BE LEARNED FROM THE PROPHETS
    HEEDING GOD'S WORD BRINGS JOY... NOT TEARS

BECOME LIKE LITTLE CHILDREN

"TRULY I TELL YOU, UNLESS YOU CHANGE AND BECOME LIKE LITTLE CHILDREN, YOU WILL NEVER ENTER THE KINGDOM OF HEAVEN." (MAT 18:3)

ATTRIBUTES OF A <u>CHILD</u> IN CHRIST:

CRAVES MILK (1PETER 2:1,2)
…RID YOURSELVES OF ALL MALICE AND ALL DECEIT, HYPROCRISY, ENVY AND SLANDER OF EVERY KIND. LIKE NEWBORN BABIES, CRAVE SPIRITUAL MILK, SO THAT BY IT YOU MAY GROW UP IN YOUR SALVATION.

FORGIVING (EPH 4:32)
BE KIND AND COMPASSIONATE TO ONE ANOTHER, FORGIVING EACH OTHER, JUST AS IN CHRIST GOD FORGAVE YOU.

DEPENDENT (JOHN 15:5)
I AM THE VINE; YOU ARE THE BRANCHES. IF YOU REMAIN IN ME, YOU WILL BEAR MUCH FRUIT; APART FROM ME YOU CAN DO NOTHING.

PERSISTENT (MATT 7:7)
ASK AND IT WILL BE GIVEN TO YOU; SEEK AND YOU WILL FIND; KNOCK AND THE DOOR WILL BE OPENED TO YOU.

SEEKS APPROVAL /FAITHFUL (MATT 25:21)
…WELL DONE, GOOD AND FAITHFUL SERVANT. YOU HAVE BEEN FAITHFUL WITH A FEW THINGS; I WILL PUT YOU IN CHARGE OF MANY THINGS. (continued)

AFFECTIONATE (JOHN 13:34)
...LOVE ONE ANOTHER. AS I HAVE LOVED YOU, SO YOU MUST
LOVE ONE ANOTHER.

CHEERFUL/PLAYFUL (PRO 17:22)
A CHEERFUL HEART IS GOOD MEDICINE; BUT A CRUSHED SPIRIT
DRIES UP THE BONES.

TRUSTWORTHY/BELIEVING (MATT 7:9)
WHICH OF YOU, IF YOUR SON ASKS FOR BREAD, WILL GIVE HIM A
STONE?

APPRECIATIVE (1 THESS (5:18)
...GIVE THANKS IN ALL CIRCUMSTANCES FOR THIS IS GOD"S WILL
FOR YOU IN CHRIST J

IMAGINATIVE (EPH 3:20)
...NOW TO HIM WHO IS ABLE TO DO IMMEASURABLY MORE THAN
ALL WE ASK OR IMAGINE, ACCORDING TO HIS POWER THAT IS AT
WORK WITHIN US...

NON-JUDGMENTAL (MATT 7:1)
DO NOT JUDGE, OR YOU WILL BE JUDGED

NO WORRIES (MATT 6:25, 32B, 33)
...DO NOT WORRY ABOUT YOUR LIFE...YOUR HEAVENLY FATHER
KNOWS THAT YOU NEED THEM (FOOD, DRINK, CLOTHING)...BUT
SEEK FIRST THE KINGDOM AND HIS RIGHTOUSNESS, AND ALL
THESE THINGS WILL BE GIVEN TO YOU AS WELL

IT'S A BEAUTIFUL DAY IN THE NEIGHBORHOOD

I NEVER KNOW WHAT EACH DAY WILL BRING
BUT TO JESUS, MY LORD, HIS PRAISES I'LL SING
WHEN I TRUST HIM TO HELP ME TO DO AS I SHOULD
IT'S ALWAYS A " BEAUTIFUL DAY IN THE NEIGHBORHOOD"

IT'S TIME TO "WAKE" (CALL ON) THE LORD

JESUS AND HIS DISCIPLES
BOARDED A BOAT ON THE LAKE
HE WANTED TO GO TO THE OTHER SIDE
WHILE SAILING HE TOOK A BREAK

AS JESUS LAY THERE, SLEEPING
A STORM BEGAN TO BREW
THE DISCIPLES DID NOT WAKE JESUS
THINKING THEY KNEW WHAT TO DO

THE BOAT BEGAN FILLING WITH WATER
THEY BAILED AS FAST AS THEY COULD
THEY TRIED THEIR BEST TO KEEP AFLOAT
BUT THEIR EFFORTS WERE DOING NO GOOD

DESPERATION BEGAN TO TAKE OVER
THOUGH THEY TRIED WITH ALL OF THEIR MIGHT
THEY CAME TO THE REALIZATION
THAT THEY WERE LOSING THE FIGHT

THEY WERE DOING THE BEST THEY COULD
BUT THEIR BEST WAS NOT GOOD ENOUGH
THIS WAS ONE OF THOSE TIMES IN THEIR LIFE
WHEN THE GOING WAS JUST WAY TOO TOUGH

SOON THEY CAME TO REALIZE
THIS COULD BE THEIR FINAL HOUR
THEY HUMBLED THEMSELVES AND FACED THE TRUTH
THEY NEEDED A GREATER POWER

THEY REACHED THAT POINT IN THEIR LIFE
WHEN THEY WERE OF ONE ACCORD
THEY TURNED TO HIM WHO WAS SLEEPING
IT WAS TIME TO WAKE THE LORD

JESUS REBUKED THE WIND AND THE RAIN
INSTANTLY THE STORM DID CEASE
HE QUESTIONED THEM, "WHERE IS YOUR FAITH"
THEY MARVELED AND WERE AT PEACE

THOUGH STORMS MAY COME INTO OUR LIVES
NOT CALMED BY MIGHT OR WORD
WE MUST ADMIT OUR WEAKNESS AND HUMBLE OURSELVES
KNOWING IT'S TIME TO "WAKE" THE LORD

MATTHEW CHAPTER SEVEN

LORD,

I DON'T WANT TO BE A JUDGE
  OF OTHERS' MOTIVES I AM NOT SURE
I WILL LEAVE JUDGING THEM UP TO YOU
  AND PRAY THAT MY MOTIVES ARE PURE

BLIND ME TO THE SPECK IN THE EYE OF OTHERS
  HELP ME SEE THEM AS YOU DO
I DESIRE TO REMOVE THE BEAM IN MY EYE
  AND HELP OTHERS TO FOLLOW YOU

GIVE TO ME YOUR DISCERNMENT
  TO KNOW WHO TRULY LOVES YOU
THAT THE PEARLS YOU HAVE ENTRUSTED TO ME
  ARE SHARED ONLY WITH THOSE WHO DO

MAY I ONLY REQUEST THOSE THINGS
  THAT YOU CONSIDER "GOOD"
I NEVER WANT TO ASK AMISS
  BUT ONLY FOR WHAT I SHOULD

HELP ME REMEMBER THE GOLDEN RULE
  KNOWING WE REAP WHATEVER WE SOW
KEEP ME ON THE STRAIGHT AND NARROW
  AND WHEN I STRAY – LET ME KNOW

WHEN I CALL YOU, "LORD, LORD..."
  KNOW THAT I AM SINCERE
LIVING TO DO YOUR FATHER'S WILL
  EACH DAY YOU KEEP ME HERE

I DON'T WANT TO BE THAT FOOLISH MAN
  WHO BUILT HIS HOUSE UPON THE SAND
BUT ANCHORED ON YOU, MY ROCK, MY LORD
  NO MATTER WHAT - I'LL STAND

THERE HAVE BEEN TIMES...

BUT BECAUSE YOU SAID...

"MASTER, WE'VE WORKED HARD ALL NIGHT AND HAVEN'T
CAUGHT ANYTHING.
BUT BECAUSE YOU SAY SO, I WILL LET DOWN THE NETS." **LK 5:5**

THERE HAVE BEEN TIMES WHEN I FELT LONELY
EVEN WHEN I WASN'T ALONE
BUT BECAUSE YOU SAID, "NEVER WILL I LEAVE YOU" **DEUT 31:6**
I KNEW I WAS NOT ON MY OWN

THERE HAVE BEEN TIMES WHEN PROBLEMS OVERWHELMED ME
I DID NOT KNOW WHERE TO START
BUT BECAUSE YOU SAID, "MY YOKE IS EASY" **MATT 11:30**
I KNEW I JUST HAD TO DO MY PART

THERE HAVE BEEN TIMES WHEN I WAS GIVING UP HOPE
I DID NOT HAVE A SOLUTION
BUT BECAUSE YOU SAID, "IF YOU HAVE FAITH" **MATT 17:20**
I KNEW THERE WAS A RESOLUTION

THERE HAVE BEEN TIMES WHEN I WAS AT A LOSS
I KNEW NOT WHAT I SHOULD SAY
BUT BECAUSE YOU SAID, "I WILL GIVE YOU THE WORDS" **LK 21:15**
I KNEW IN THE SPIRIT TO PRAY

THERE HAVE BEEN TIMES WHEN I THOUGHT I WOULD "LOSE IT"
MY PATIENCE WAS PUT TO THE TEST
BUT BECAUSE YOU SAID, "BE ANGRY AND SIN NOT" **EPH 4:26,27**
I KNEW SAYING LESS WOULD BE BEST

THERE HAVE BEEN TIMES WHEN IT WAS HARD TO SHOW LOVE
TO THOSE WHO HURT AND ACCUSE
BUT BECAUSE YOU SAID, "LOVE YOUR ENEMIES" **MATT 5:44**
I KNEW JUST WHAT I WAS TO DO

(continued)

THERE HAVE BEEN TIMES WHEN THE NEEDS SEEMED TOO MANY
AND I BEGAN TO FRET
BUT BECAUSE YOU SAID, "I WILL PROVIDE"   **GEN 50:21**
I KNEW ALL OUR NEEDS WOULD BE MET

THERE HAVE BEEN TIMES WHEN I HAVE BEEN TEMPTED
AND NEARLY DID WHAT I SHOULD NOT
BUT BECAUSE YOU SAID, "YOU WILL PROVIDE A WAY OUT"
ICOR 10:13
I KNEW I SHOULD CAPTURE MY THOUGHTS

I AM

I AM YOUR LIGHT IN THE DARKNESS
YOUR CALM IN THE STORM
YOUR PEACE WHEN IN TURMOIL
YOUR FRIEND WHEN FORLORN

MY REFRAIN
 I AM WHO "I AM"
ALWAYS WAS AND WILL BE
I AM HERE FOR YOU,
WILL YOU SPEND TIME WITH ME?

I PROVIDE REST WHEN YOU'RE WEARY
STRENGTH WHEN YOU'RE WEAK
TURN YOUR MOURNING TO GLADNESS
KNOW YOUR HEART WHEN YOU SPEAK

I SHOW MERCY WITHOUT MEASURE
FORGIVE WHEN YOU REPENT
FOR MY GRACE IS SUFFICIENT
MY PATIENCE NEVER SPENT

I AM YOUR BANNER OF LOVE
YOUR SHIELD AND PROTECTOR
YOUR DEFENSE AND REFUGE
YOUR STRONG AND HIGH TOWER

I AM YOUR SOURCE OF COMFORT
PROVIDER OF YOUR NEEDS
HEALER OF YOUR BROKEN HEART
AND ALL SICKNESS AND DISEASE

I LOVE YOU WITHOUT WAVERING
I WILL NOT BETRAY YOUR TRUST
IN MY PRESENCE YOU WILL FIND JOY
MY WAYS ARE TRUE AND JUST

(continued)

I KNOW THE PLANS I HAVE FOR YOU
PLANS FOR A GLORIOUS END
I'LL LEAD YOU TO STILL WATERS
BE YOUR COMFORTER AND FRIEND

I FREE YOU FROM OPPRESSION
I'VE CONQUERED YOUR ENEMY
I WILL STAY CLOSER THAN A BROTHER
YOU CAN PUT YOUR FAITH IN ME

I AM YOUR BREAD OF LIFE
YOUR SOURCE OF LIVING WATERS
SUPPLIER AND PROVIDER
FOR YOU... MY SONS AND DAUGHTERS

I LIGHTEN YOUR HEAVY HEART
MY YOKE WILL NOT BRING SORROW
I'LL BE THE LIFTER OF YOUR HEAD
AND GIVE YOU HOPE FOR EACH TOMORROW

God said to Moses, "I AM WHO I AM. (Ex 3:14)

NEVER TOO YOUNG
(ECCL 12:1,2)

MY CHILD, NOW IS THE TIME TO SEEK ME OUT
EVEN AS YOUR FUTURE TAKES SHAPE
SPEND TIME WITH ME TO GAIN COUNSEL AND WISDOM
TO HELP WITH THE CHOICES YOU'LL MAKE

YOU SAY YOU'RE STILL YOUNG AND HAVE PLENTY OF TIME
YOU HAVE A LOT OF LIVING TO DO
YOU'RE JUST TOO BUSY TO MAKE TIME FOR ME
THE WORLD IS WAITING FOR YOU

NOW YOU ARE MANAGING THINGS ON YOUR OWN
LIFE IS EASY - THERE IS NOTHING TO IT
BUT IF THINGS GET TOUGH AND YOU'RE IN A BIND
YOU'LL CALL ME TO HELP YOU THROUGH IT

MAY I SUGGEST THAT NOW IS THE TIME
TO GAIN THE WISDOM YOU'LL NEED
TO PREPARE FOR WHATEVER YOU'LL ENCOUNTER IN LIFE
AND KNOWING HOW TO PROCEED

THE GREATER THE DISTANCE BETWEEN YOU AND ME
THE MORE ELUSIVE I'LL SEEM
MAKE TIME NOW AND DRAW NEAR TO ME
I'LL BE A TRUE FRIEND INDEED

THE BEST TIME TO PREPARE FOR THE DARKNESS
IS WHILE YOU STILL HAVE THE LIGHT
SO WHEN YOU CAN'T SEE WHAT LIES AHEAD
YOU'LL KEEP WALKING BY FAITH - NOT SIGHT

GOD IS FAITHFUL

UNTO GOD'S FAITHFUL, LIFE IS CHANGED – NOT TAKEN AWAY!

UNTO GOD'S FAITHFUL, HE IS REVEALED	PS 18:25
FAITHFULLY CONFIRMING HIS PRESENCE WITHIN	2COR 13:5
WITH HIS FAITHFUL GOD PERSEVERES	PS 31:23
WHEREVER THEY ARE, HE IS WITH THEM	DEUT 31:6

THOUGH THEY BE SHAKEN, THEY'RE NEVER FORSAKEN	PS 31:23
GOD'S FAITHFUL POSSESS A WARRIORS MIGHT	PS 89:19
HE IS THEIR PROTECTOR; HE GUARDS THEIR LIVES	PRO 2:8
THEY ARE NEVER OUT OF HIS SIGHT	PS 101:6

GOD'S FAITHFUL ARE REWARDED AND RICHLY BLESSED	PRO 28:20
AND AS THEY HUMBLE THEMSELVES AND PRAY	
ALL THOSE WHO HAVE BEEN FOUND FAITHFUL	
WILL FIND LIFE IS CHANGED – NOT TAKEN AWAY!	

PUT IT ALL IN PERSPECTIVE

OR

NOT A VICTIM OF CIRCUMSTANCES

LORD, THANK YOU FOR REMINDING ME TODAY THAT CIRCUMSTANCES DO NOT DETERMINE WHETHER I AM HAVING A GOOD, BAD OR MEDIOCRE DAY. REGARDLESS OF WHAT I MAY ENCOUNTER, YOU ARE STILL MY SAVIOR, I AM YOUR CHILD, YOUR LOVE IS UNCONDITIONAL, AND I AM JUST PASSING THROUGH THIS LIFE ON MY WAY TO BEING WITH YOU.

IT'S OKAY IF I DON'T KNOW EVERYTHING. IT'S OKAY IF I DON'T HAVE ALL THE ANSWERS. I DON'T ALWAYS NEED AN EXPLANATION. MANY OF THE PROBLEMS I ENCOUNTER AND THINGS I DEAL WITH ON A DAILY BASIS ARE SOMETIMES OF MY OWN DOING – BUT I KNOW YOU WILL EVEN HELP ME DEAL WITH THEM.

I AM GRATEFUL FOR YOUR GRACE AND YOUR PATIENCE. I ALSO KNOW THERE ARE NO COINCIDENCES. NO MATTER WHAT HAPPENS, YOU HAVE A WAY OF USING THE OCCASION TO TEACH A LESSON. YOU CAN BRING SOMEONE IN MY PATH TO HELP ME, OR SHOW ME. IT IS ANOTHER OPPORTUNITY TO ACKNOWLEDGE Y-O-U. YOU ARE EVER-PRESENT AND EVER-READY, AND I AM NEVER ALONE TO MAKE IT THROUGH THE DAY. THANKS!

THE LORD SAYS:

YOU ARE PARDONED
     YOU ARE FREE (ROMANS 6:18)
WHOM I HAVE FREED
     IS FREE INDEED (JOHN 8:36)
ONCE SLAVES TO SIN
     YOU'VE BEEN REDEEMED (ROMANS 7:25)
I'VE PAID YOUR DEBT
     COME FOLLOW ME (MATTHEW 19:21)

FREE OF FAULT
     NO GUILT TO FACE (1JN 1:9 /ROM 8:1)
NOT UNDER LAW
     BUT UNDER GRACE (ROMANS 6:15)
YOU ARE RIGHTEOUS
     IN MY SIGHT (2 CORINTHIANS 5:21)
NOT OF DARKNESS
     BUT OFTHE LIGHT (MATTHEW 5:14 / EPHESIANS 5:8)

NO BURDEN TOO GREAT
     FOR US TO BEAR (PSALMS 81:6, 7)
WHEN YOU CALL ME
     I'LL BE THERE (PSALMS 17:6 / ISAIAH 59:21)
MY POWER, MY STRENGTH
     WILL SEE YOU THROUGH (ISAIAH 40:31)
WHATEVER NEEDS DONE
     I WILL DO (MATTHEW 6:8, 25)

LET MY SPIRIT
     BE YOUR GUIDE (JOHN 16:13)
PUT ASIDE
     ALL SELFISH PRIDE (PROVERBS 16:18)
WHEN SEEKING ANSWERS
     IN ME CONFIDE (MATTHEW 7:7)
I'LL MEET YOUR NEEDS
     YOU WON'T BE DENIED (JOHN 14:14)

COME, FELLOWSHIP WITH ME
LET US COMMUNE TOGETHER
IN MY PRESENCE IS HOPE AND PEACE
AND A LOVE THAT LASTS FOREVER

Joseph R. DiCostanzo

Section 6

From a Fig Leaf to a Righteous Robe

FROM A FIG LEAVE TO A RIGHTEOUS ROBE

For many years I felt the shame for offending God by the things I did, things I said and things I thought.

I knew I was a sinner, and I knew I did not want to spend eternity in hell.

Rom 3:23-24
...for all have sinned and fall short of the glory of God, and all are justified freely by his grace through the redemption that came by Christ Jesus.

Rom 6:23
For the wages of sin is death, but the gift of God is eternal life in Christ Jesus our Lord.

Confessing my sins to a priest seemed to be my only option, but there was always the dread of spending time in purgatory. Purgatory, according to the Catholic teaching, is a place of temporal punishment. Purgatory is for souls that died in a state of grace where they are made ready for heaven.

When I was older, I learned of gaining indulgences. Indulgences could be used to reduce the time I had to would spend in purgatory. An indulgence is the remission of the temporal punishment, which would have been inflicted for confessed sin. Indulgences do not take away the guilt.

I could also "earn" indulgences for others. I participated in many novenas. Novenas were nine days of prayer and /or fasting to gain indulgences for the remission of punishment due to sins committed by me and/or those who have died. I often wondered how many novenas I had to attend, prayers I had to say and candles I had to light to "release" me, and those I prayed for from purgatory. What if those I prayed for were no longer in purgatory? Would anybody be offering indulgences on my behalf?

(continued)

Because the Lord knew my heart, he sent individuals into my life who introduced me to His Word - the Bible. Questions I had about confession, purgatory, indulgences, and which church, was the right one were answered in His Word. I realized that my salvation (and getting to heaven) had nothing to do with religion or a denomination but my salvation had everything to do with my relationship with God's Son - Jesus Christ. It was true that I had to confess my offenses against God. But my confession was not to be to a priest. My confession was to be to the One whom I offended, the only One with the power to forgive sins.

1Tim 2:5
...for there is one God and one mediator between God and mankind, the man Jesus Christ.

I learned that my salvation was in recognizing Christ as my Savior and making him the Lord of my life.

Rom 10:9,-10
If you declare with your mouth, "Jesus is Lord", and believe in your heart that God raised him from the dead, you will be saved. For it is with the heart that you believe and are justified, and it is with your mouth that you profess your faith and are saved.

What a relief to know Christ paid the penalty for my sins!

Col 1:21,22
Once you were alienated from God and were enemies in your minds because of your evil behavior. But now he has reconciled you by Christ's physical body through death to present you holy in His sight, without blemish and free from accusation

Forgiveness was for real, complete and forever!

Ps 103:12
... as far as the east is from the west, so far has He removed our transgressions

God forgives and forgets

(continued)

1Cor 1:8
…he will also keep you firm to the end, so that you will be blameless on the day of our Lord, Jesus Christ.

My salvation was assured when I freely died to self, recognized Christ as my savior and submitted myself to His authority. I could not save myself.

Eph 2:8,9
For by grace you have been saved through faith - and this is not from yourselves, it is the gift of God - not of works, so that no one can boast.

I no longer fear god's wrath. I am not condemned to hell - or purgatory!
Rom 8:1
Therefore, there is now no condemnation for those who are in Christ Jesus. The penalty for my sins has been paid in full.

1Cor 6:20; 7:22
For you are bought with a price: therefore glorify God in your body, and you and your spirit, which are God's… for the one who was a slave when called to faith in the Lord is the Lord's freed person.

I have dedicated my life to his service. That's right - I am his servant

Jn 12:26
Whoever serves me must follow me; and where I am, my servant also will be. my Father will honor the one who serves me

Rom 6:22
But now that you have been set free from sin, and have become slaves of God, the benefit you reap leads to holiness, and the result is eternal life.

I remember reading in Genesis 3:7 that Adam and Eve "sewed fig leaves together and made coverings for themselves" because of their guilt. And in Isaiah 1:18 it says "though your sins be as scarlet, they shall be as white as snow".

No more hiding behind fig leafs! No more shame!

Rom 5:8
…but God demonstrates his love for us in this: while we were yet sinners, Christ died for us.

(continued)

I have been made righteous. Forget the fig leaf! I am clothed in His righteousness.

Isa 61:10
I greatly delight in the Lord; my soul rejoices in my God. For he has clothed me with garments of salvation and arranged me in a robe of His righteousness, as a bridegroom adorns his head like a priest, and as a bride adorns herself with her jewels.

Thank you, Lord, for paying my debt which I could never repay.
Thank you for your love, joy and peace that I experience every day.
I pray You will find me to be faithful.

May I honor you all the days of my life. I pray others are drawn to You by your Holy Spirit that lives in me. May your grace abound in my life. I pray these things in the precious name of my Lord and Savior, Jesus Christ.

Amen.

Section 7

Recollections Of Dad and Mom

MY DAD

I am son number two in a family of six - counting mom and dad. Dad was a quiet and soft-spoken man who was highly respected by all who knew him. He was a kind, patient man with a gentle spirit who had a difficult time saying "no" when others asked him for a favor.

Dad was a talented bricklayer in and out of Crucible Steel where he was a foreman of a brick "gang". He displayed his talent on many homes in the area when he was asked to do the brickwork.

I enjoyed spending time with my Dad. If Dad was working in the garden I was there. When I was too small to use the shovel or pitchfork, I held the seeds and planted them. I know I caused him more work by my "helping" him, but he would always take the time to show me what to do and how to do it.

One day, while cleaning brush and tall grass from the far end of our property, we disturbed a wasp nest. They chased my Dad and I all the way to the house. I remember Dad used wet tobacco (he smoked a pipe and Marsh Wheeling cigars) on all our stings to soothe the itch and pain, it worked!

Dad often played ball with us in our large yard, and raced us up and down the street alongside our property. On summer nights, he would sometimes surprise us with a trip to Hanks Frozen Custard. That was a real treat!

If there was a baby or young child around, you could bet that Dad would be holding and/or playing with him or her.

He was the one my brothers, sister and I would go to when we wanted permission to do something or go somewhere, because he usually said "yes". That worked until mom got upset with his giving in to us. Then he started saying, "go ask your mother".

I attended Presentation Catholic Church in Midland, Pa. where I also attended Catholic school through the eighth grade. Beginning in the fourth grade, I sang in the children's choir. I had to be at church for 7:30 mass on weekdays. I rode with my Dad when he left for work. He had to be at work at 8 o'clock, but left early to get me to church. He was pleased that I was in the choir. I enjoyed riding with dad much more than riding the school bus.

I cannot ever recall a time when Dad was in a bad mood. He did not get really upset about anything - at least when us children were around. He seemed to take everything in stride. When Mom was upset with him about something, he would just listen to her. I don't even remember him responding to mom in any manner other than a soft-spoken, polite tone of voice. I don't recall his speaking negatively about others - even when he was wronged. Maybe that is why I enjoyed being around him. He was always soft-spoken, kind and patient. Dad really demonstrated many of the attributes of our heavenly father.

He encouraged us to do well in school so we would not end up working in the steel mill. He would like to have completed a higher level of education. Dad's father had an accident at the mill and could no longer work to support the family. Dad quit school (I believe he was in the eighth grade.) to go to work in the mill. He tried to complete his high school education via a correspondence course, but was not able to because of the lack of time and money.

He was pleased that I was accepted to Washington and Jefferson College. When I voiced concern for the costs involved, he told me not to worry. He said he would do whatever was necessary to make sure I made it to graduation..

Dad's parents and sisters would often call on him to pray for them when they were not well. He would lay hands on them and silently pray. When I asked what he prayed, he said he would tell me sometime. He did show me a prayer he had memorized when he ministered to members of his family. (I now know I do not need to recite a particular prayer, but God answers any heartfelt prayer.) I remember the day a "prayer cloth" came in the mail at dad's request from Oral Roberts ministry. We were told Catholics should not associate with others, who are not Catholic, but we did not question my dad.

He was a faithful, hard worker who rarely missed a day of work, and it was difficult for him when he was diagnosed with tuberculosis, silicosis and emphysema and had to go to a sanitarium in Cresson, PA, because he was contagious. His lungs were badly damaged. He spent six months in the sanitarium until he was no longer contagious with TB.

I made frequent trips home from college on weekends so we could visit him. Mom wanted to be there as much as possible. They had never been separated for that long before this. When discharged from the hospital, the doctor said there was nothing more they could do for him. He said to keep him as comfortable as possible, and his heart would eventually fail because of the stress on his heart - three months to a year they said.

Dad passed away at the beginning of my senior year at W & J. I wish he were there to see me graduate. But that was not meant to be. He passed away about six months later - August 26, 1965- at the beginning of my senior year at Washington and Jefferson College.

I believe Dad had a personal relationship with Jesus Christ. After he passed away, we found a well-read Bible in the desk where he kept his personal papers, bills, etc. as Catholics we were never encouraged to read the Bible. He had scripture references and verses written on bits of paper in the Bible. One of the notes we found read "unto thy faithful, oh lord, life is changed not taken away". We had this inscribed on his tombstone in Beaver Cemetery. We also had a rose put on the marker, because it was his favorite flower.

One of the compliments that always meant the most to me was when others would say, "you remind me of your father. You are a lot like him."

My prayer is that I will always honor my Dad and my heavenly Father.

Joseph R. DiCostanzo

MY MOM

Mom was a faithful wife and dedicated mother. She was an excellent homemaker: clean house, home-cooked meals, fresh-baked bread, pizza and rolls, fresh pasta, home-canned fruits and vegetables and clean clothes. Home was a pleasant place to be. All our family, friends, classmates and neighbors enjoyed coming to our home. Holiday parties and special events were usually held at our home.

Oh, yes! - Mom was the disciplinarian in our home. She made sure we did our chores, and she was the one who used the paddle when she felt it was necessary (even if we didn't).

Every summer and into the fall she would spend hours canning enough fruits and vegetables to last until the next harvest. They were stored in the "wine cellar" (formerly called the coal cellar). Very few canned goods were purchased at the store.

Mom never left you wondering what she was thinking - she usually let you know. I think she verbalized what others were thinking. I remember when Dad, long before he got sick, finally convinced mom to get a drivers license. She was driving with a permit, and we were all in the car. We were behind a stopped bus. Dad told Mom to put on her signal and pass the bus, but she did not want to. When she finally made the decision to pass, she did not clear the bus and hit the bumper putting a slight dent in the car. She refused to drive after that incident, and I don't recall if she ever got her license. I know she never drove the car.

Mom and Dad did just about everything together (shopping, visiting, wedding receptions, etc.) - and us four children went along as well. I recall their declining invitations to wedding receptions if children were not included. When dad was in the hospital and sanitarium, Mom appeared to be so lonely. I knew she was hurting inside, but there was nothing anyone could do. Several times I saw her wiping tears from her eyes while trying to appear to be strong while keeping up with all that needed to be done around the house. When Dad got home from the hospital, the only time Mom would leave the house was to go grocery shopping.

Dad never wanted Mom to work. But after he passed away, she could not stand staying around the house. We had friends who helped her get a job at Westinghouse Electric assembling breakers. It was not easy work, but she adjusted very well. She would get up about 5 a.m. every day and walk about a block to catch a ride with some coworkers. It was good for her to have a job. She made new friends. It got her out of the house where she said she would sometimes hear dad calling her.

110

We knew it would be good for mom to have a companion, but we had some reservations about whom she eventually married. He was a good companion for mom. She traveled more with him than she had all her life before meeting him. Several years later he was diagnosed with lung cancer and passed away.

Mom fell and needed an elbow replacement. She later needed surgery for carpal tunnel when she began losing feeling in her hands. She later had neck surgery when she began losing feeling in her legs. While mom was staying at Regina's after her surgery, she accepted Jesus Christ as her Savior. It was a Tupperware dealer who had the honor of leading her to the Lord.

Mom stayed with my sister and brother-in-law for a while and was later admitted to an assisted living facility near my brother and sister-in-law in Pittsburgh.

While Mom was in the assisted living facility in Pittsburgh, we invited her to stay with us in Kansas for brief periods of time. She really enjoyed being with us and having a change of scenery. When it was time for her to return to Pittsburgh, she was already looking forward to her next trip back to be with us. Her visits were usually during the Christmas holiday, and we tried to offer as many enjoyable experiences as possible while she was with us.

Mom passed away on April 8, 1999

Joseph R. DiCostanzo